C-812 CAREER EXAMINATION SERIES

This is your
PASSBOOK for...

Traffic Control Inspector

Test Preparation Study Guide
Questions & Answers

COPYRIGHT NOTICE

This book is SOLELY intended for, is sold ONLY to, and its use is RESTRICTED to individual, bona fide applicants or candidates who qualify by virtue of having seriously filed applications for appropriate license, certificate, professional and/or promotional advancement, higher school matriculation, scholarship, or other legitimate requirements of education and/or governmental authorities.

This book is NOT intended for use, class instruction, tutoring, training, duplication, copying, reprinting, excerption, or adaptation, etc., by:

1) Other publishers
2) Proprietors and/or Instructors of "Coaching" and/or Preparatory Courses
3) Personnel and/or Training Divisions of commercial, industrial, and governmental organizations
4) Schools, colleges, or universities and/or their departments and staffs, including teachers and other personnel
5) Testing Agencies or Bureaus
6) Study groups which seek by the purchase of a single volume to copy and/or duplicate and/or adapt this material for use by the group as a whole without having purchased individual volumes for each of the members of the group
7) Et al.

Such persons would be in violation of appropriate Federal and State statutes.

PROVISION OF LICENSING AGREEMENTS – Recognized educational, commercial, industrial, and governmental institutions and organizations, and others legitimately engaged in educational pursuits, including training, testing, and measurement activities, may address request for a licensing agreement to the copyright owners, who will determine whether, and under what conditions, including fees and charges, the materials in this book may be used them. In other words, a licensing facility exists for the legitimate use of the material in this book on other than an individual basis. However, it is asseverated and affirmed here that the material in this book CANNOT be used without the receipt of the express permission of such a licensing agreement from the Publishers. Inquiries re licensing should be addressed to the company, attention rights and permissions department.

All rights reserved, including the right of reproduction in whole or in part, in any form or by any means, electronic or mechanical, including photocopying, recording, or by any information storage and retrieval system, without permission in writing from the Publisher.

Copyright © 2025 by
National Learning Corporation

212 Michael Drive, Syosset, NY 11791
(516) 921-8888 • www.passbooks.com
E-mail: info@passbooks.com

PASSBOOK® SERIES

THE *PASSBOOK® SERIES* has been created to prepare applicants and candidates for the ultimate academic battlefield – the examination room.

At some time in our lives, each and every one of us may be required to take an examination – for validation, matriculation, admission, qualification, registration, certification, or licensure.

Based on the assumption that every applicant or candidate has met the basic formal educational standards, has taken the required number of courses, and read the necessary texts, the *PASSBOOK® SERIES* furnishes the one special preparation which may assure passing with confidence, instead of failing with insecurity. Examination questions – together with answers – are furnished as the basic vehicle for study so that the mysteries of the examination and its compounding difficulties may be eliminated or diminished by a sure method.

This book is meant to help you pass your examination provided that you qualify and are serious in your objective.

The entire field is reviewed through the huge store of content information which is succinctly presented through a provocative and challenging approach – the question-and-answer method.

A climate of success is established by furnishing the correct answers at the end of each test.

You soon learn to recognize types of questions, forms of questions, and patterns of questioning. You may even begin to anticipate expected outcomes.

You perceive that many questions are repeated or adapted so that you can gain acute insights, which may enable you to score many sure points.

You learn how to confront new questions, or types of questions, and to attack them confidently and work out the correct answers.

You note objectives and emphases, and recognize pitfalls and dangers, so that you may make positive educational adjustments.

Moreover, you are kept fully informed in relation to new concepts, methods, practices, and directions in the field.

You discover that you are actually taking the examination all the time: you are preparing for the examination by "taking" an examination, not by reading extraneous and/or supererogatory textbooks.

In short, this PASSBOOK®, used directedly, should be an important factor in helping you to pass your test.

TRAFFIC CONTROL INSPECTOR

DUTIES AND RESPONSIBILITIES
Under supervision, makes inspections of traffic conditions to regulate and control traffic; performs related work.

EXAMPLES OF TYPICAL TASK
Investigates complaints on such matters as heavy trucking, constant parking, lack of traffic signals or loading zones. Checks volume of traffic visibility, grading and line of street. Makes recommendations on need for traffic signs, traffic signals, channelization markings, or other traffic control devices. Makes studies of effect of establishment of one-way street systems. Studies accident reports and makes observations at scene of accident to determine causal pattern. Makes surveys of parking conditions and facilities. Investigates requests for establishment or elimination of taxicab stands. Prepares reports and makes sketches of observed conditions.

TESTS
The written test will be of the multiple-choice type and may include questions on characteristics of traffic, traffic rules and regulations, traffic signs and signals, traffic accidents, traffic studies, parking, safety, and other related areas.

HOW TO TAKE A TEST

I. YOU MUST PASS AN EXAMINATION

A. *WHAT EVERY CANDIDATE SHOULD KNOW*

Examination applicants often ask us for help in preparing for the written test. What can I study in advance? What kinds of questions will be asked? How will the test be given? How will the papers be graded?

As an applicant for a civil service examination, you may be wondering about some of these things. Our purpose here is to suggest effective methods of advance study and to describe civil service examinations.

Your chances for success on this examination can be increased if you know how to prepare. Those "pre-examination jitters" can be reduced if you know what to expect. You can even experience an adventure in good citizenship if you know why civil service exams are given.

B. *WHY ARE CIVIL SERVICE EXAMINATIONS GIVEN?*

Civil service examinations are important to you in two ways. As a citizen, you want public jobs filled by employees who know how to do their work. As a job seeker, you want a fair chance to compete for that job on an equal footing with other candidates. The best-known means of accomplishing this two-fold goal is the competitive examination.

Exams are widely publicized throughout the nation. They may be administered for jobs in federal, state, city, municipal, town or village governments or agencies.

Any citizen may apply, with some limitations, such as the age or residence of applicants. Your experience and education may be reviewed to see whether you meet the requirements for the particular examination. When these requirements exist, they are reasonable and applied consistently to all applicants. Thus, a competitive examination may cause you some uneasiness now, but it is your privilege and safeguard.

C. *HOW ARE CIVIL SERVICE EXAMS DEVELOPED?*

Examinations are carefully written by trained technicians who are specialists in the field known as "psychological measurement," in consultation with recognized authorities in the field of work that the test will cover. These experts recommend the subject matter areas or skills to be tested; only those knowledges or skills important to your success on the job are included. The most reliable books and source materials available are used as references. Together, the experts and technicians judge the difficulty level of the questions.

Test technicians know how to phrase questions so that the problem is clearly stated. Their ethics do not permit "trick" or "catch" questions. Questions may have been tried out on sample groups, or subjected to statistical analysis, to determine their usefulness.

Written tests are often used in combination with performance tests, ratings of training and experience, and oral interviews. All of these measures combine to form the best-known means of finding the right person for the right job.

II. HOW TO PASS THE WRITTEN TEST

A. NATURE OF THE EXAMINATION

To prepare intelligently for civil service examinations, you should know how they differ from school examinations you have taken. In school you were assigned certain definite pages to read or subjects to cover. The examination questions were quite detailed and usually emphasized memory. Civil service exams, on the other hand, try to discover your present ability to perform the duties of a position, plus your potentiality to learn these duties. In other words, a civil service exam attempts to predict how successful you will be. Questions cover such a broad area that they cannot be as minute and detailed as school exam questions.

In the public service similar kinds of work, or positions, are grouped together in one "class." This process is known as *position-classification*. All the positions in a class are paid according to the salary range for that class. One class title covers all of these positions, and they are all tested by the same examination.

B. FOUR BASIC STEPS

1) Study the announcement

How, then, can you know what subjects to study? Our best answer is: "Learn as much as possible about the class of positions for which you've applied." The exam will test the knowledge, skills and abilities needed to do the work.

Your most valuable source of information about the position you want is the official exam announcement. This announcement lists the training and experience qualifications. Check these standards and apply only if you come reasonably close to meeting them.

The brief description of the position in the examination announcement offers some clues to the subjects which will be tested. Think about the job itself. Review the duties in your mind. Can you perform them, or are there some in which you are rusty? Fill in the blank spots in your preparation.

Many jurisdictions preview the written test in the exam announcement by including a section called "Knowledge and Abilities Required," "Scope of the Examination," or some similar heading. Here you will find out specifically what fields will be tested.

2) Review your own background

Once you learn in general what the position is all about, and what you need to know to do the work, ask yourself which subjects you already know fairly well and which need improvement. You may wonder whether to concentrate on improving your strong areas or on building some background in your fields of weakness. When the announcement has specified "some knowledge" or "considerable knowledge," or has used adjectives like "beginning principles of..." or "advanced ... methods," you can get a clue as to the number and difficulty of questions to be asked in any given field. More questions, and hence broader coverage, would be included for those subjects which are more important in the work. Now weigh your strengths and weaknesses against the job requirements and prepare accordingly.

3) Determine the level of the position

Another way to tell how intensively you should prepare is to understand the level of the job for which you are applying. Is it the entering level? In other words, is this the position in which beginners in a field of work are hired? Or is it an intermediate or advanced level? Sometimes this is indicated by such words as "Junior" or "Senior" in the class title. Other jurisdictions use Roman numerals to designate the level – Clerk I, Clerk II, for example. The word "Supervisor" sometimes appears in the title. If the level is not indicated by the title, check the description of duties. Will you be working under very close supervision, or will you have responsibility for independent decisions in this work?

4) Choose appropriate study materials

Now that you know the subjects to be examined and the relative amount of each subject to be covered, you can choose suitable study materials. For beginning level jobs, or even advanced ones, if you have a pronounced weakness in some aspect of your training, read a modern, standard textbook in that field. Be sure it is up to date and has general coverage. Such books are normally available at your library, and the librarian will be glad to help you locate one. For entry-level positions, questions of appropriate difficulty are chosen – neither highly advanced questions, nor those too simple. Such questions require careful thought but not advanced training.

If the position for which you are applying is technical or advanced, you will read more advanced, specialized material. If you are already familiar with the basic principles of your field, elementary textbooks would waste your time. Concentrate on advanced textbooks and technical periodicals. Think through the concepts and review difficult problems in your field.

These are all general sources. You can get more ideas on your own initiative, following these leads. For example, training manuals and publications of the government agency which employs workers in your field can be useful, particularly for technical and professional positions. A letter or visit to the government department involved may result in more specific study suggestions, and certainly will provide you with a more definite idea of the exact nature of the position you are seeking.

III. KINDS OF TESTS

Tests are used for purposes other than measuring knowledge and ability to perform specified duties. For some positions, it is equally important to test ability to make adjustments to new situations or to profit from training. In others, basic mental abilities not dependent on information are essential. Questions which test these things may not appear as pertinent to the duties of the position as those which test for knowledge and information. Yet they are often highly important parts of a fair examination. For very general questions, it is almost impossible to help you direct your study efforts. What we can do is to point out some of the more common of these general abilities needed in public service positions and describe some typical questions.

1) General information

Broad, general information has been found useful for predicting job success in some kinds of work. This is tested in a variety of ways, from vocabulary lists to questions about current events. Basic background in some field of work, such as sociology or economics, may be sampled in a group of questions. Often these are principles which have become familiar to most persons through exposure rather than through formal training. It is difficult to advise you how to study for these questions; being alert to the world around you is our best suggestion.

2) Verbal ability

An example of an ability needed in many positions is verbal or language ability. Verbal ability is, in brief, the ability to use and understand words. Vocabulary and grammar tests are typical measures of this ability. Reading comprehension or paragraph interpretation questions are common in many kinds of civil service tests. You are given a paragraph of written material and asked to find its central meaning.

3) Numerical ability

Number skills can be tested by the familiar arithmetic problem, by checking paired lists of numbers to see which are alike and which are different, or by interpreting charts and graphs. In the latter test, a graph may be printed in the test booklet which you are asked to use as the basis for answering questions.

4) Observation

A popular test for law-enforcement positions is the observation test. A picture is shown to you for several minutes, then taken away. Questions about the picture test your ability to observe both details and larger elements.

5) Following directions

In many positions in the public service, the employee must be able to carry out written instructions dependably and accurately. You may be given a chart with several columns, each column listing a variety of information. The questions require you to carry out directions involving the information given in the chart.

6) Skills and aptitudes

Performance tests effectively measure some manual skills and aptitudes. When the skill is one in which you are trained, such as typing or shorthand, you can practice. These tests are often very much like those given in business school or high school courses. For many of the other skills and aptitudes, however, no short-time preparation can be made. Skills and abilities natural to you or that you have developed throughout your lifetime are being tested.

Many of the general questions just described provide all the data needed to answer the questions and ask you to use your reasoning ability to find the answers. Your best preparation for these tests, as well as for tests of facts and ideas, is to be at your physical and mental best. You, no doubt, have your own methods of getting into an exam-taking mood and keeping "in shape." The next section lists some ideas on this subject.

IV. KINDS OF QUESTIONS

Only rarely is the "essay" question, which you answer in narrative form, used in civil service tests. Civil service tests are usually of the short-answer type. Full instructions for answering these questions will be given to you at the examination. But in case this is your first experience with short-answer questions and separate answer sheets, here is what you need to know:

1) Multiple-choice Questions

Most popular of the short-answer questions is the "multiple choice" or "best answer" question. It can be used, for example, to test for factual knowledge, ability to solve problems or judgment in meeting situations found at work.

A multiple-choice question is normally one of three types—
- It can begin with an incomplete statement followed by several possible endings. You are to find the one ending which *best* completes the statement, although some of the others may not be entirely wrong.
- It can also be a complete statement in the form of a question which is answered by choosing one of the statements listed.

- It can be in the form of a problem – again you select the best answer.

Here is an example of a multiple-choice question with a discussion which should give you some clues as to the method for choosing the right answer:

When an employee has a complaint about his assignment, the action which will *best* help him overcome his difficulty is to
   A. discuss his difficulty with his coworkers
   B. take the problem to the head of the organization
   C. take the problem to the person who gave him the assignment
   D. say nothing to anyone about his complaint

In answering this question, you should study each of the choices to find which is best. Consider choice "A" – Certainly an employee may discuss his complaint with fellow employees, but no change or improvement can result, and the complaint remains unresolved. Choice "B" is a poor choice since the head of the organization probably does not know what assignment you have been given, and taking your problem to him is known as "going over the head" of the supervisor. The supervisor, or person who made the assignment, is the person who can clarify it or correct any injustice. Choice "C" is, therefore, correct. To say nothing, as in choice "D," is unwise. Supervisors have and interest in knowing the problems employees are facing, and the employee is seeking a solution to his problem.

2) True/False Questions

The "true/false" or "right/wrong" form of question is sometimes used. Here a complete statement is given. Your job is to decide whether the statement is right or wrong.

SAMPLE: A roaming cell-phone call to a nearby city costs less than a non-roaming call to a distant city.

This statement is wrong, or false, since roaming calls are more expensive.
This is not a complete list of all possible question forms, although most of the others are variations of these common types. You will always get complete directions for answering questions. Be sure you understand *how* to mark your answers – ask questions until you do.

V. RECORDING YOUR ANSWERS

Computer terminals are used more and more today for many different kinds of exams.
For an examination with very few applicants, you may be told to record your answers in the test booklet itself. Separate answer sheets are much more common. If this separate answer sheet is to be scored by machine – and this is often the case – it is highly important that you mark your answers correctly in order to get credit.
An electronic scoring machine is often used in civil service offices because of the speed with which papers can be scored. Machine-scored answer sheets must be marked with a pencil, which will be given to you. This pencil has a high graphite content which responds to the electronic scoring machine. As a matter of fact, stray dots may register as answers, so do not let your pencil rest on the answer sheet while you are pondering the correct answer. Also, if your pencil lead breaks or is otherwise defective, ask for another.

Since the answer sheet will be dropped in a slot in the scoring machine, be careful not to bend the corners or get the paper crumpled.

The answer sheet normally has five vertical columns of numbers, with 30 numbers to a column. These numbers correspond to the question numbers in your test booklet. After each number, going across the page are four or five pairs of dotted lines. These short dotted lines have small letters or numbers above them. The first two pairs may also have a "T" or "F" above the letters. This indicates that the first two pairs only are to be used if the questions are of the true-false type. If the questions are multiple choice, disregard the "T" and "F" and pay attention only to the small letters or numbers.

Answer your questions in the manner of the sample that follows:

32. The largest city in the United States is
    A. Washington, D.C.
    B. New York City
    C. Chicago
    D. Detroit
    E. San Francisco

1) Choose the answer you think is best. (New York City is the largest, so "B" is correct.)
2) Find the row of dotted lines numbered the same as the question you are answering. (Find row number 32)
3) Find the pair of dotted lines corresponding to the answer. (Find the pair of lines under the mark "B.")
4) Make a solid black mark between the dotted lines.

VI. BEFORE THE TEST

Common sense will help you find procedures to follow to get ready for an examination. Too many of us, however, overlook these sensible measures. Indeed, nervousness and fatigue have been found to be the most serious reasons why applicants fail to do their best on civil service tests. Here is a list of reminders:

- Begin your preparation early – Don't wait until the last minute to go scurrying around for books and materials or to find out what the position is all about.
- Prepare continuously – An hour a night for a week is better than an all-night cram session. This has been definitely established. What is more, a night a week for a month will return better dividends than crowding your study into a shorter period of time.
- Locate the place of the exam – You have been sent a notice telling you when and where to report for the examination. If the location is in a different town or otherwise unfamiliar to you, it would be well to inquire the best route and learn something about the building.
- Relax the night before the test – Allow your mind to rest. Do not study at all that night. Plan some mild recreation or diversion; then go to bed early and get a good night's sleep.
- Get up early enough to make a leisurely trip to the place for the test – This way unforeseen events, traffic snarls, unfamiliar buildings, etc. will not upset you.
- Dress comfortably – A written test is not a fashion show. You will be known by number and not by name, so wear something comfortable.

- Leave excess paraphernalia at home – Shopping bags and odd bundles will get in your way. You need bring only the items mentioned in the official notice you received; usually everything you need is provided. Do not bring reference books to the exam. They will only confuse those last minutes and be taken away from you when in the test room.
- Arrive somewhat ahead of time – If because of transportation schedules you must get there very early, bring a newspaper or magazine to take your mind off yourself while waiting.
- Locate the examination room – When you have found the proper room, you will be directed to the seat or part of the room where you will sit. Sometimes you are given a sheet of instructions to read while you are waiting. Do not fill out any forms until you are told to do so; just read them and be prepared.
- Relax and prepare to listen to the instructions
- If you have any physical problem that may keep you from doing your best, be sure to tell the test administrator. If you are sick or in poor health, you really cannot do your best on the exam. You can come back and take the test some other time.

VII. AT THE TEST

The day of the test is here and you have the test booklet in your hand. The temptation to get going is very strong. Caution! There is more to success than knowing the right answers. You must know how to identify your papers and understand variations in the type of short-answer question used in this particular examination. Follow these suggestions for maximum results from your efforts:

1) Cooperate with the monitor

The test administrator has a duty to create a situation in which you can be as much at ease as possible. He will give instructions, tell you when to begin, check to see that you are marking your answer sheet correctly, and so on. He is not there to guard you, although he will see that your competitors do not take unfair advantage. He wants to help you do your best.

2) Listen to all instructions

Don't jump the gun! Wait until you understand all directions. In most civil service tests you get more time than you need to answer the questions. So don't be in a hurry. Read each word of instructions until you clearly understand the meaning. Study the examples, listen to all announcements and follow directions. Ask questions if you do not understand what to do.

3) Identify your papers

Civil service exams are usually identified by number only. You will be assigned a number; you must not put your name on your test papers. Be sure to copy your number correctly. Since more than one exam may be given, copy your exact examination title.

4) Plan your time

Unless you are told that a test is a "speed" or "rate of work" test, speed itself is usually not important. Time enough to answer all the questions will be provided, but this does not mean that you have all day. An overall time limit has been set. Divide the total time (in minutes) by the number of questions to determine the approximate time you have for each question.

5) Do not linger over difficult questions

If you come across a difficult question, mark it with a paper clip (useful to have along) and come back to it when you have been through the booklet. One caution if you do this – be sure to skip a number on your answer sheet as well. Check often to be sure that you have not lost your place and that you are marking in the row numbered the same as the question you are answering.

6) Read the questions

Be sure you know what the question asks! Many capable people are unsuccessful because they failed to *read* the questions correctly.

7) Answer all questions

Unless you have been instructed that a penalty will be deducted for incorrect answers, it is better to guess than to omit a question.

8) Speed tests

It is often better NOT to guess on speed tests. It has been found that on timed tests people are tempted to spend the last few seconds before time is called in marking answers at random – without even reading them – in the hope of picking up a few extra points. To discourage this practice, the instructions may warn you that your score will be "corrected" for guessing. That is, a penalty will be applied. The incorrect answers will be deducted from the correct ones, or some other penalty formula will be used.

9) Review your answers

If you finish before time is called, go back to the questions you guessed or omitted to give them further thought. Review other answers if you have time.

10) Return your test materials

If you are ready to leave before others have finished or time is called, take ALL your materials to the monitor and leave quietly. Never take any test material with you. The monitor can discover whose papers are not complete, and taking a test booklet may be grounds for disqualification.

VIII. EXAMINATION TECHNIQUES

1) Read the general instructions carefully. These are usually printed on the first page of the exam booklet. As a rule, these instructions refer to the timing of the examination; the fact that you should not start work until the signal and must stop work at a signal, etc. If there are any *special* instructions, such as a choice of questions to be answered, make sure that you note this instruction carefully.

2) When you are ready to start work on the examination, that is as soon as the signal has been given, read the instructions to each question booklet, underline any key words or phrases, such as *least, best, outline, describe* and the like. In this way you will tend to answer as requested rather than discover on reviewing your paper that you *listed without describing*, that you selected the *worst* choice rather than the *best* choice, etc.

3) If the examination is of the objective or multiple-choice type – that is, each question will also give a series of possible answers: A, B, C or D, and you are called upon to select the best answer and write the letter next to that answer on your answer paper – it is advisable to start answering each question in turn. There may be anywhere from 50 to 100 such questions in the three or four hours allotted and you can see how much time would be taken if you read through all the questions before beginning to answer any. Furthermore, if you come across a question or group of questions which you know would be difficult to answer, it would undoubtedly affect your handling of all the other questions.

4) If the examination is of the essay type and contains but a few questions, it is a moot point as to whether you should read all the questions before starting to answer any one. Of course, if you are given a choice – say five out of seven and the like – then it is essential to read all the questions so you can eliminate the two that are most difficult. If, however, you are asked to answer all the questions, there may be danger in trying to answer the easiest one first because you may find that you will spend too much time on it. The best technique is to answer the first question, then proceed to the second, etc.

5) Time your answers. Before the exam begins, write down the time it started, then add the time allowed for the examination and write down the time it must be completed, then divide the time available somewhat as follows:
   - If 3-1/2 hours are allowed, that would be 210 minutes. If you have 80 objective-type questions, that would be an average of 2-1/2 minutes per question. Allow yourself no more than 2 minutes per question, or a total of 160 minutes, which will permit about 50 minutes to review.
   - If for the time allotment of 210 minutes there are 7 essay questions to answer, that would average about 30 minutes a question. Give yourself only 25 minutes per question so that you have about 35 minutes to review.

6) The most important instruction is to *read each question* and make sure you know what is wanted. The second most important instruction is to *time yourself properly* so that you answer every question. The third most important instruction is to *answer every question*. Guess if you have to but include something for each question. Remember that you will receive no credit for a blank and will probably receive some credit if you write something in answer to an essay question. If you guess a letter – say "B" for a multiple-choice question – you may have guessed right. If you leave a blank as an answer to a multiple-choice question, the examiners may respect your feelings but it will not add a point to your score. Some exams may penalize you for wrong answers, so in such cases *only*, you may not want to guess unless you have some basis for your answer.

7) Suggestions
   a. Objective-type questions
      1. Examine the question booklet for proper sequence of pages and questions
      2. Read all instructions carefully
      3. Skip any question which seems too difficult; return to it after all other questions have been answered
      4. Apportion your time properly; do not spend too much time on any single question or group of questions

5. Note and underline key words – *all, most, fewest, least, best, worst, same, opposite,* etc.
6. Pay particular attention to negatives
7. Note unusual option, e.g., unduly long, short, complex, different or similar in content to the body of the question
8. Observe the use of "hedging" words – *probably, may, most likely,* etc.
9. Make sure that your answer is put next to the same number as the question
10. Do not second-guess unless you have good reason to believe the second answer is definitely more correct
11. Cross out original answer if you decide another answer is more accurate; do not erase until you are ready to hand your paper in
12. Answer all questions; guess unless instructed otherwise
13. Leave time for review

b. Essay questions
1. Read each question carefully
2. Determine exactly what is wanted. Underline key words or phrases.
3. Decide on outline or paragraph answer
4. Include many different points and elements unless asked to develop any one or two points or elements
5. Show impartiality by giving pros and cons unless directed to select one side only
6. Make and write down any assumptions you find necessary to answer the questions
7. Watch your English, grammar, punctuation and choice of words
8. Time your answers; don't crowd material

8) Answering the essay question

Most essay questions can be answered by framing the specific response around several key words or ideas. Here are a few such key words or ideas:

M's: manpower, materials, methods, money, management
P's: purpose, program, policy, plan, procedure, practice, problems, pitfalls, personnel, public relations

a. Six basic steps in handling problems:
1. Preliminary plan and background development
2. Collect information, data and facts
3. Analyze and interpret information, data and facts
4. Analyze and develop solutions as well as make recommendations
5. Prepare report and sell recommendations
6. Install recommendations and follow up effectiveness

b. Pitfalls to avoid
1. *Taking things for granted* – A statement of the situation does not necessarily imply that each of the elements is necessarily true; for example, a complaint may be invalid and biased so that all that can be taken for granted is that a complaint has been registered

2. *Considering only one side of a situation* – Wherever possible, indicate several alternatives and then point out the reasons you selected the best one
3. *Failing to indicate follow up* – Whenever your answer indicates action on your part, make certain that you will take proper follow-up action to see how successful your recommendations, procedures or actions turn out to be
4. *Taking too long in answering any single question* – Remember to time your answers properly

IX. AFTER THE TEST

Scoring procedures differ in detail among civil service jurisdictions although the general principles are the same. Whether the papers are hand-scored or graded by machine we have described, they are nearly always graded by number. That is, the person who marks the paper knows only the number – never the name – of the applicant. Not until all the papers have been graded will they be matched with names. If other tests, such as training and experience or oral interview ratings have been given, scores will be combined. Different parts of the examination usually have different weights. For example, the written test might count 60 percent of the final grade, and a rating of training and experience 40 percent. In many jurisdictions, veterans will have a certain number of points added to their grades.

After the final grade has been determined, the names are placed in grade order and an eligible list is established. There are various methods for resolving ties between those who get the same final grade – probably the most common is to place first the name of the person whose application was received first. Job offers are made from the eligible list in the order the names appear on it. You will be notified of your grade and your rank as soon as all these computations have been made. This will be done as rapidly as possible.

People who are found to meet the requirements in the announcement are called "eligibles." Their names are put on a list of eligible candidates. An eligible's chances of getting a job depend on how high he stands on this list and how fast agencies are filling jobs from the list.

When a job is to be filled from a list of eligibles, the agency asks for the names of people on the list of eligibles for that job. When the civil service commission receives this request, it sends to the agency the names of the three people highest on this list. Or, if the job to be filled has specialized requirements, the office sends the agency the names of the top three persons who meet these requirements from the general list.

The appointing officer makes a choice from among the three people whose names were sent to him. If the selected person accepts the appointment, the names of the others are put back on the list to be considered for future openings.

That is the rule in hiring from all kinds of eligible lists, whether they are for typist, carpenter, chemist, or something else. For every vacancy, the appointing officer has his choice of any one of the top three eligibles on the list. This explains why the person whose name is on top of the list sometimes does not get an appointment when some of the persons lower on the list do. If the appointing officer chooses the second or third eligible, the No. 1 eligible does not get a job at once, but stays on the list until he is appointed or the list is terminated.

X. HOW TO PASS THE INTERVIEW TEST

The examination for which you applied requires an oral interview test. You have already taken the written test and you are now being called for the interview test – the final part of the formal examination.

You may think that it is not possible to prepare for an interview test and that there are no procedures to follow during an interview. Our purpose is to point out some things you can do in advance that will help you and some good rules to follow and pitfalls to avoid while you are being interviewed.

What is an interview supposed to test?

The written examination is designed to test the technical knowledge and competence of the candidate; the oral is designed to evaluate intangible qualities, not readily measured otherwise, and to establish a list showing the relative fitness of each candidate – as measured against his competitors – for the position sought. Scoring is not on the basis of "right" and "wrong," but on a sliding scale of values ranging from "not passable" to "outstanding." As a matter of fact, it is possible to achieve a relatively low score without a single "incorrect" answer because of evident weakness in the qualities being measured.

Occasionally, an examination may consist entirely of an oral test – either an individual or a group oral. In such cases, information is sought concerning the technical knowledges and abilities of the candidate, since there has been no written examination for this purpose. More commonly, however, an oral test is used to supplement a written examination.

Who conducts interviews?

The composition of oral boards varies among different jurisdictions. In nearly all, a representative of the personnel department serves as chairman. One of the members of the board may be a representative of the department in which the candidate would work. In some cases, "outside experts" are used, and, frequently, a businessman or some other representative of the general public is asked to serve. Labor and management or other special groups may be represented. The aim is to secure the services of experts in the appropriate field.

However the board is composed, it is a good idea (and not at all improper or unethical) to ascertain in advance of the interview who the members are and what groups they represent. When you are introduced to them, you will have some idea of their backgrounds and interests, and at least you will not stutter and stammer over their names.

What should be done before the interview?

While knowledge about the board members is useful and takes some of the surprise element out of the interview, there is other preparation which is more substantive. It *is* possible to prepare for an oral interview – in several ways:

1) Keep a copy of your application and review it carefully before the interview

This may be the only document before the oral board, and the starting point of the interview. Know what education and experience you have listed there, and the sequence and dates of all of it. Sometimes the board will ask you to review the highlights of your experience for them; you should not have to hem and haw doing it.

2) Study the class specification and the examination announcement

Usually, the oral board has one or both of these to guide them. The qualities, characteristics or knowledges required by the position sought are stated in these documents. They offer valuable clues as to the nature of the oral interview. For example, if the job involves supervisory responsibilities, the announcement will usually indicate that knowledge of modern supervisory methods and the qualifications of the candidate as a supervisor will be tested. If so, you can expect such questions, frequently in the form of a hypothetical situation which you are expected to solve. NEVER go into an oral without knowledge of the duties and responsibilities of the job you seek.

3) Think through each qualification required

Try to visualize the kind of questions you would ask if you were a board member. How well could you answer them? Try especially to appraise your own knowledge and background in each area, *measured against the job sought*, and identify any areas in which you are weak. Be critical and realistic – do not flatter yourself.

4) Do some general reading in areas in which you feel you may be weak

For example, if the job involves supervision and your past experience has NOT, some general reading in supervisory methods and practices, particularly in the field of human relations, might be useful. Do NOT study agency procedures or detailed manuals. The oral board will be testing your understanding and capacity, not your memory.

5) Get a good night's sleep and watch your general health and mental attitude

You will want a clear head at the interview. Take care of a cold or any other minor ailment, and of course, no hangovers.

What should be done on the day of the interview?

Now comes the day of the interview itself. Give yourself plenty of time to get there. Plan to arrive somewhat ahead of the scheduled time, particularly if your appointment is in the fore part of the day. If a previous candidate fails to appear, the board might be ready for you a bit early. By early afternoon an oral board is almost invariably behind schedule if there are many candidates, and you may have to wait. Take along a book or magazine to read, or your application to review, but leave any extraneous material in the waiting room when you go in for your interview. In any event, relax and compose yourself.

The matter of dress is important. The board is forming impressions about you – from your experience, your manners, your attitude, and your appearance. Give your personal appearance careful attention. Dress your best, but not your flashiest. Choose conservative, appropriate clothing, and be sure it is immaculate. This is a business interview, and your appearance should indicate that you regard it as such. Besides, being well groomed and properly dressed will help boost your confidence.

Sooner or later, someone will call your name and escort you into the interview room. *This is it.* From here on you are on your own. It is too late for any more preparation. But remember, you asked for this opportunity to prove your fitness, and you are here because your request was granted.

What happens when you go in?

The usual sequence of events will be as follows: The clerk (who is often the board stenographer) will introduce you to the chairman of the oral board, who will introduce you to the other members of the board. Acknowledge the introductions before you sit down. Do not be surprised if you find a microphone facing you or a stenotypist sitting by. Oral interviews are usually recorded in the event of an appeal or other review.

Usually the chairman of the board will open the interview by reviewing the highlights of your education and work experience from your application – primarily for the benefit of the other members of the board, as well as to get the material into the record. Do not interrupt or comment unless there is an error or significant misinterpretation; if that is the case, do not hesitate. But do not quibble about insignificant matters. Also, he will usually ask you some question about your education, experience or your present job – partly to get you to start talking and to establish the interviewing "rapport." He may start the actual questioning, or turn it over to one of the other members. Frequently, each member undertakes the questioning on a particular area, one in which he is perhaps most competent, so you can expect each member to participate in the examination. Because time is limited, you may also expect some rather abrupt switches in the direction the questioning takes, so do not be upset by it. Normally, a board member will not pursue a single line of questioning unless he discovers a particular strength or weakness.

After each member has participated, the chairman will usually ask whether any member has any further questions, then will ask you if you have anything you wish to add. Unless you are expecting this question, it may floor you. Worse, it may start you off on an extended, extemporaneous speech. The board is not usually seeking more information. The question is principally to offer you a last opportunity to present further qualifications or to indicate that you have nothing to add. So, if you feel that a significant qualification or characteristic has been overlooked, it is proper to point it out in a sentence or so. Do not compliment the board on the thoroughness of their examination – they have been sketchy, and you know it. If you wish, merely say, "No thank you, I have nothing further to add." This is a point where you can "talk yourself out" of a good impression or fail to present an important bit of information. Remember, *you close the interview yourself*.

The chairman will then say, "That is all, Mr. _____, thank you." Do not be startled; the interview is over, and quicker than you think. Thank him, gather your belongings and take your leave. Save your sigh of relief for the other side of the door.

How to put your best foot forward

Throughout this entire process, you may feel that the board individually and collectively is trying to pierce your defenses, seek out your hidden weaknesses and embarrass and confuse you. Actually, this is not true. They are obliged to make an appraisal of your qualifications for the job you are seeking, and they want to see you in your best light. Remember, they must interview all candidates and a non-cooperative candidate may become a failure in spite of their best efforts to bring out his qualifications. Here are 15 suggestions that will help you:

1) Be natural – Keep your attitude confident, not cocky

If you are not confident that you can do the job, do not expect the board to be. Do not apologize for your weaknesses, try to bring out your strong points. The board is interested in a positive, not negative, presentation. Cockiness will antagonize any board member and make him wonder if you are covering up a weakness by a false show of strength.

2) Get comfortable, but don't lounge or sprawl

Sit erectly but not stiffly. A careless posture may lead the board to conclude that you are careless in other things, or at least that you are not impressed by the importance of the occasion. Either conclusion is natural, even if incorrect. Do not fuss with your clothing, a pencil or an ashtray. Your hands may occasionally be useful to emphasize a point; do not let them become a point of distraction.

3) Do not wisecrack or make small talk

This is a serious situation, and your attitude should show that you consider it as such. Further, the time of the board is limited – they do not want to waste it, and neither should you.

4) Do not exaggerate your experience or abilities

In the first place, from information in the application or other interviews and sources, the board may know more about you than you think. Secondly, you probably will not get away with it. An experienced board is rather adept at spotting such a situation, so do not take the chance.

5) If you know a board member, do not make a point of it, yet do not hide it

Certainly you are not fooling him, and probably not the other members of the board. Do not try to take advantage of your acquaintanceship – it will probably do you little good.

6) Do not dominate the interview

Let the board do that. They will give you the clues – do not assume that you have to do all the talking. Realize that the board has a number of questions to ask you, and do not try to take up all the interview time by showing off your extensive knowledge of the answer to the first one.

7) Be attentive

You only have 20 minutes or so, and you should keep your attention at its sharpest throughout. When a member is addressing a problem or question to you, give him your undivided attention. Address your reply principally to him, but do not exclude the other board members.

8) Do not interrupt

A board member may be stating a problem for you to analyze. He will ask you a question when the time comes. Let him state the problem, and wait for the question.

9) Make sure you understand the question

Do not try to answer until you are sure what the question is. If it is not clear, restate it in your own words or ask the board member to clarify it for you. However, do not haggle about minor elements.

10) Reply promptly but not hastily

A common entry on oral board rating sheets is "candidate responded readily," or "candidate hesitated in replies." Respond as promptly and quickly as you can, but do not jump to a hasty, ill-considered answer.

11) Do not be peremptory in your answers

A brief answer is proper – but do not fire your answer back. That is a losing game from your point of view. The board member can probably ask questions much faster than you can answer them.

12) Do not try to create the answer you think the board member wants

He is interested in what kind of mind you have and how it works – not in playing games. Furthermore, he can usually spot this practice and will actually grade you down on it.

13) Do not switch sides in your reply merely to agree with a board member

Frequently, a member will take a contrary position merely to draw you out and to see if you are willing and able to defend your point of view. Do not start a debate, yet do not surrender a good position. If a position is worth taking, it is worth defending.

14) Do not be afraid to admit an error in judgment if you are shown to be wrong

The board knows that you are forced to reply without any opportunity for careful consideration. Your answer may be demonstrably wrong. If so, admit it and get on with the interview.

15) Do not dwell at length on your present job

The opening question may relate to your present assignment. Answer the question but do not go into an extended discussion. You are being examined for a *new* job, not your present one. As a matter of fact, try to phrase ALL your answers in terms of the job for which you are being examined.

Basis of Rating

Probably you will forget most of these "do's" and "don'ts" when you walk into the oral interview room. Even remembering them all will not ensure you a passing grade. Perhaps you did not have the qualifications in the first place. But remembering them will help you to put your best foot forward, without treading on the toes of the board members.

Rumor and popular opinion to the contrary notwithstanding, an oral board wants you to make the best appearance possible. They know you are under pressure – but they also want to see how you respond to it as a guide to what your reaction would be under the pressures of the job you seek. They will be influenced by the degree of poise you display, the personal traits you show and the manner in which you respond.

ABOUT THIS BOOK

This book contains tests divided into Examination Sections. Go through each test, answering every question in the margin. We have also attached a sample answer sheet at the back of the book that can be removed and used. At the end of each test look at the answer key and check your answers. On the ones you got wrong, look at the right answer choice and learn. Do not fill in the answers first. Do not memorize the questions and answers, but understand the answer and principles involved. On your test, the questions will likely be different from the samples. Questions are changed and new ones added. If you understand these past questions you should have success with any changes that arise. Tests may consist of several types of questions. We have additional books on each subject should more study be advisable or necessary for you. Finally, the more you study, the better prepared you will be. This book is intended to be the last thing you study before you walk into the examination room. Prior study of relevant texts is also recommended. NLC publishes some of these in our Fundamental Series. Knowledge and good sense are important factors in passing your exam. Good luck also helps. So now study this Passbook, absorb the material contained within and take that knowledge into the examination. Then do your best to pass that exam.

EXAMINATION SECTION

EXAMINATION SECTION
TEST 1

DIRECTIONS: Each question or incomplete statement is followed by several suggested answers or completions. Select the one that BEST answers the question or completes the statement. *PRINT THE LETTER OF THE CORRECT ANSWER IN THE SPACE AT THE RIGHT.*

1. Under conditions of rain and fog, headlights MUST be turned on if visibility is *less than*   1.____

    A. 100 feet
    B. 500 feet
    C. 1,000 feet
    D. 1/4 of a mile

2. If a blowout occurs while a vehicle is moving, the driver SHOULD   2.____

    A. hold tightly onto the steering wheel and immediately apply steady foot pressure to the brake pedal
    B. hold tightly onto the steering wheel and turn off the roadway as soon as the blowout occurs, stopping the vehicle on the shoulder area
    C. start tapping the brake pedal with his foot, sound his horn to warn others, and move into the slow-moving lane immediately
    D. hold tightly onto the steering wheel, steer straight ahead, and ease up on the accelerator

3. Which of the following is NOT a correct action to take after parking on a shoulder of a highway?   3.____

    A. Turn on the emergency lights
    B. Have all occupants stay inside the vehicle
    C. Open the hood of the car
    D. Fasten a white cloth to the door handle or radio antenna

4. It is officially recommended that drivers stay behind cars in front of them a distance of at least one car length for every ten miles per hour of speed.
The PRINCIPAL reason for this is to   4.____

    A. increase roadway capacity
    B. make it easier for cars to change lanes
    C. allow for enough distance to stop safely if the car ahead stops suddenly
    D. keep all the cars moving at the same speed

5. To *minimize* the glare from lights of oncoming cars at night, a driver should   5.____

    A. shift his eyes to the lower right side of his traffic lane
    B. blink his eyes frequently
    C. shift his eyes to the upper right side of his traffic lane
    D. use his upper beams to offset the glare

6. The number of yards in a mile is   6.____

    A. 5,280   B. 1,760   C. 880   D. 440

7. Vehicle classification data is MOST important in calculating the
   A. capacity of a roadway
   B. timing of traffic signals
   C. turnover of parking in a lot
   D. average speed of travel

8. Condition diagrams show
   A. the same information as collision diagrams plus information about vehicle classification
   B. the same information as collision diagrams plus information about vehicle speeds and traffic volumes
   C. traffic volumes only
   D. existing physical features at a location

9. Thirty miles per hour is *equivalent* to _____ feet per second.
   A. 30   B. 44   C. 60   D. 80

10. Origin and destination studies are used CHIEFLY to
    A. obtain information on travel habits
    B. collect traffic volume data
    C. estimate travel time between cities
    D. determine roadway capacities

11. The BEST way to determine the number of cars parked in an off-street parking lot during a 12-hour period is to conduct a(n)_____ study.
    A. parking occupancy   B. vehicle classification
    C. origin/destination   D. parking turnover

12. The BEST way to determine the number of vehicles that have been parked for more than 1 hour within a 1-hour parking meter area is to record the _____ every hour.
    A. color of each vehicle parked
    B. license numbers of every parked vehicle
    C. make and year of each car parked
    D. number of violations shown on the meters

13. A traffic flow map is used to show
    A. speeds along a highway in both directions and at intersections
    B. the available capacity on a highway during peak hours
    C. the traffic volumes that pass through an intersection or travel along a highway
    D. the one- and two-way street patterns in an area

14. The *running speed* on a highway is the
    A. posted speed limit
    B. length of the highway divided by the time it takes to travel the highway
    C. speed for which the highway was designed
    D. speed at a specific point along the highway as determined through a radar speed study

15. The 85 percentile speed on a given stretch of highway for a certain period of time is   15.____

    A. the speed below which 85% of all traffic travels
    B. the speed above which 85% of all traffic travels
    C. 85% of the posted speed limit
    D. 85% of the running speed

16. The *modal* speed on a highway is   16.____

    A. average speed traveled by vehicles using the highway
    B. speed value which is halfway between the highest and lowest speed recorded in a speed study
    C. average spot speed at a given station on the highway
    D. speed value occurring most frequently as recorded in a speed study

17. For a given number of lanes in a roadway, the capacity of the roadway   17.____

    A. decreases as lane widths decrease
    B. increases as lane widths decrease
    C. is not affected by lane widths
    D. is affected by lane widths only on steep grades

18. Speed and delay studies are used to   18.____

    A. determine the number of vehicles traveling above and below the speed limit
    B. establish speed limits
    C. identify locations where curb parking needs to be restricted
    D. measure the effectiveness of changes in traffic signal timing

19. The average annual daily traffic on a highway is the   19.____

    A. total yearly volume divided by the number of days in the year
    B. average weekday volume times 365
    C. average of the highest and lowest 24-hour volumes recorded during the year
    D. average 24-hour volume recorded exclusive of Saturdays, Sundays, and holidays

20. Turning movement counts at intersections are USUALLY made   20.____

    A. with the use of mechanical counters
    B. with the use of radar detectors
    C. by manual means
    D. by estimation based upon traffic flow diagrams

21. Under ideal roadway and traffic conditions, the basic capacity for uninterrupted traffic   21.____
    flow conditions foreach lane of a multi-lane roadway is _____ passenger cars per hour.

    A. 500   B. 1,000   C. 2,000   D. 4,000

22. For heavy volumes of mixed traffic, the IDEAL lane width is _____ feet.   22.____

    A. 10   B. 12   C. 14   D. 16

23. When describing highway capacity under various traffic conditions, flow, volumes, and speeds, levels of service definitions are used.
    The level of service which describes a condition on the roadway of free flow, low volume, and high speed is known as level of service

    A. A   B. B   C. C   D. D

24. The MOST efficient use of space in a rectangular or square-shaped parking lot can USUALLY be arrived at through the use of _____ parking stalls.

    A. parallel
    B. 45-degree
    C. 90-degree
    D. a combination of angle and 90-degree

25. If a single mechanical traffic counter is installed on each approach to an intersection, the data collected will NOT include

    A. peak hour volumes
    B. the total volumes through the intersection
    C. turning movements
    D. motorcycle traffic

KEY (CORRECT ANSWERS)

1. C		11. D	
2. D		12. B	
3. B		13. C	
4. C		14. B	
5. A		15. A	
6. B		16. D	
7. A		17. A	
8. D		18. D	
9. B		19. A	
10. A		20. C	

21. C
22. B
23. A
24. C
25. C

TEST 2

DIRECTIONS: Each question or incomplete statement is followed by several suggested answers or completions. Select the one that BEST answers the question or completes the statement. *PRINT THE LETTER OF THE CORRECT ANSWER IN THE SPACE AT THE RIGHT.*

Questions 1-5.

DIRECTIONS: Questions 1 through 5, inclusive, refer to Figures 1 and 2, which appear below and on the following page.

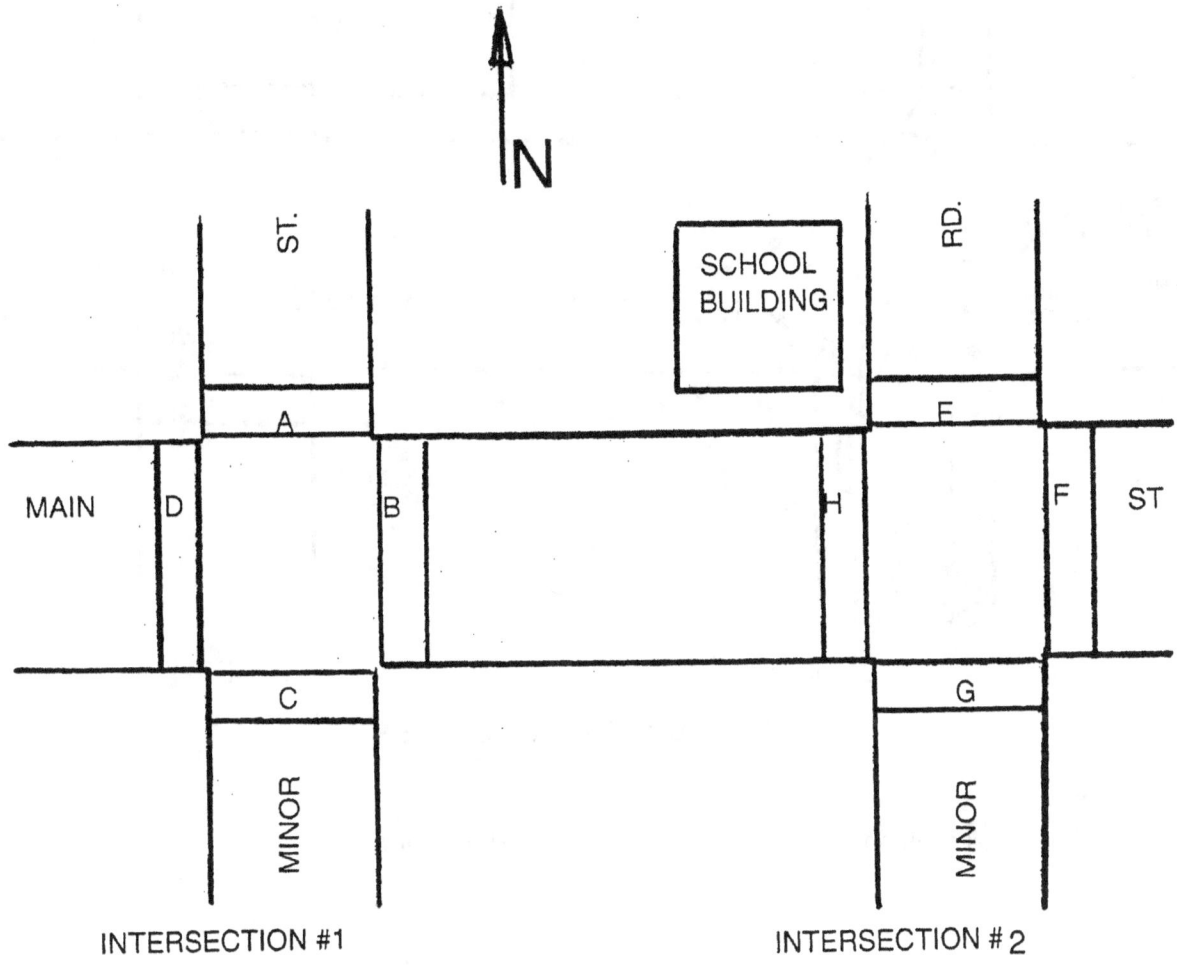

POSSIBLE CROSSWALK LOCATION

NOTES	STREET DIRECTIONS
1	Main Street Is one-way eastbound
2	Cross Street Is two-way
3	Cross Road is one-way northbound
4	Both intersections are uncontrolled

FIGURE 1

2 (#2)

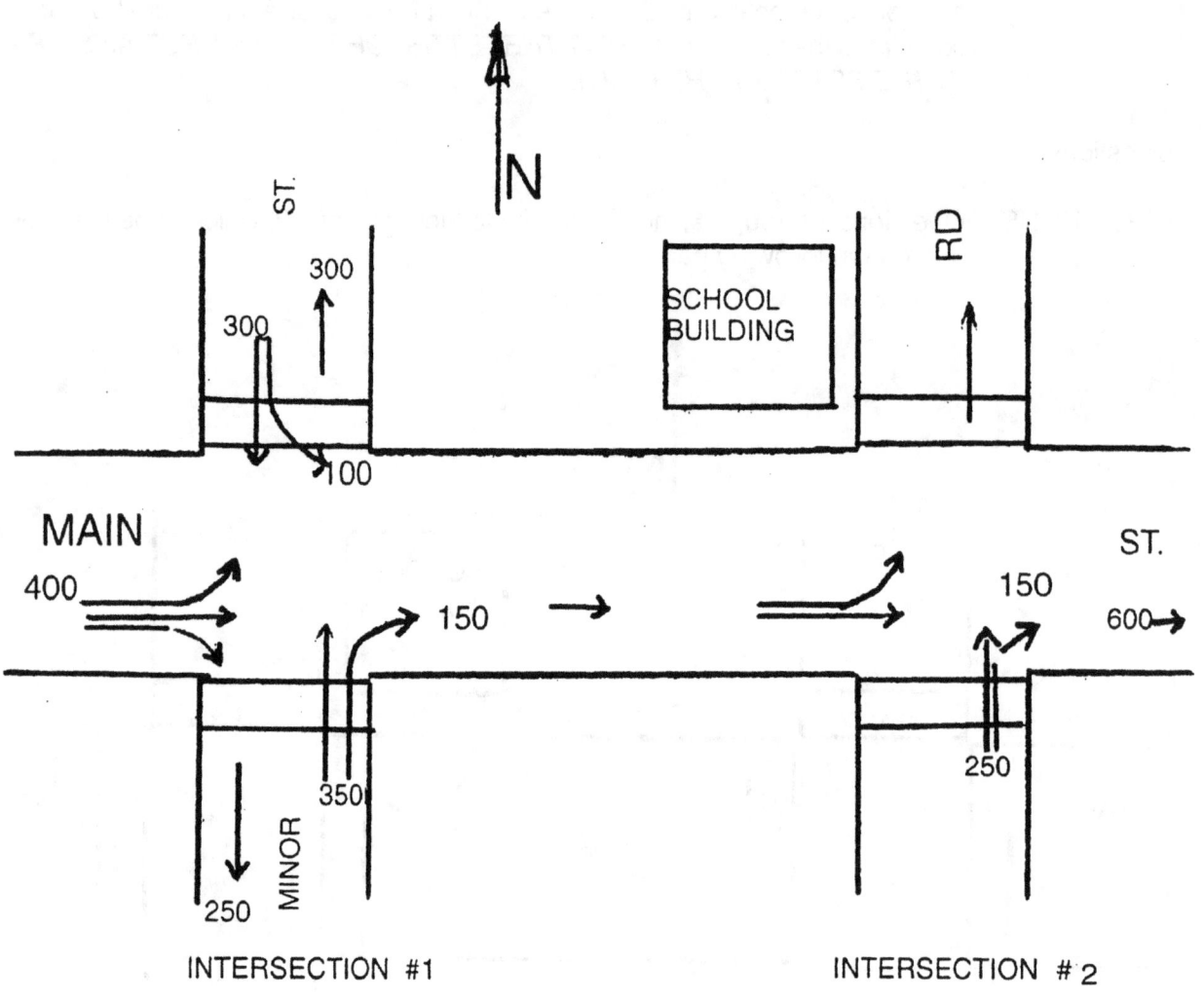

SCHOOL HOUR TRAFFIC VOLUMES

NOTE:
1   Volumes shown are for arrival and departure periods.

FIGURE 2

1. At intersection #1, the TOTAL traffic volume that crosses crosswalk B is MOST NEARLY   1.___

   A. 250   B. 350   C. 400   D. 500

2. At intersection #2, the TOTAL traffic volume that moves straight ahead at crosswalk G is   2.___
   MOST NEARLY

   A. 100   B. 150   C. 200   D. 250

3. At intersection #1, the TOTAL traffic volume that moves straight ahead at crosswalk D is   3.___
   MOST NEARLY

   A. 150   B. 200   C. 250   D. 300

4. At intersection #2, the crosswalks that should be designated as school crossings are
   A. E, F, G, H
   B. E, F, G
   C. E, F, H
   D. E, H, G

5. Assuming that only one police officer or school crossing guard can be assigned for school crossing patrol duty, the officer or guard should be assigned to intersection
   A. #1 during student arrival periods and at intersection #2 during student departure periods
   B. #2 during student arrival periods and at intersection #1 during student departure periods
   C. #1 during both arrival and departure periods
   D. #2 during both arrival and departure periods

6. In the city, the CLOSEST a car may be parked to a hydrant is _____ feet.
   A. 5   B. 10   C. 15   D. 20

7. Of the following violations, the one which would NOT be recorded as a penalty on a driver's license is
   A. failure to stop at a stop sign
   B. double parking
   C. front or rear lights not working
   D. passing a red light

8. The current trend in the manufacture of new automobiles in the United States is to
   A. give the new automobiles capacity for higher speeds
   B. make them smaller
   C. restore the running board
   D. give them disappearing front lights

9. Of the following, the statement relating to parking meter spaces adjacent to fire hydrants that is MOST NEARLY correct is they
   A. may be made shorter than others in the block
   B. must be at least 25 feet long
   C. cannot be closer than 20 feet to the hydrant
   D. may be within 10 feet of the hydrant

10. In the city, parking signs that prohibit parking are made with _____ letters on a _____ background.
    A. green; white
    B. white; green
    C. black; white
    D. red; white

11. A driver whose car is parked for 8 hours in an off-street facility where the rate is 50 cents an hour for the first 5 hours and 75 cents an hour thereafter would pay
    A. $6.00   B. $5.75   C. $4.75   D. $4.00

12. To encourage shoppers and other short-term parkers and to discourage commuters from using parking garages in the city, it would be BEST to

    A. charge a uniform high hourly rate all day
    B. charge a high rate for the first three to five hours and decrease the rate thereafter
    C. charge a lower rate for the first three hours and increase the rate sharply thereafter
    D. limit all parking to one-half hour

13. If an investigation of insufficient parking for customers at a busy post office revealed that the only six available spaces were occupied by all-day parkers, the recommended action should be to

    A. install two-hour parking signs
    B. make the area a No Parking zone
    C. do nothing because the spaces are being used
    D. install 20-minute meters

14. A street which can accommodate 40 parked trucks along both curbs is experiencing congestion problems because there are not enough lanes for through traffic. A survey reveals stores and businesses along both sides of the street and truck parking along both curbs. The total number of vehicles parked is never more than 20.
    The recommended action should be to

    A. prohibit truck parking at all times along one curb
    B. prohibit truck parking for the first half of the day along one curb and the second half of the day along the other curb
    C. prohibit parking on alternate days along each curb
    D. establish loading zones mid-block along each curb

15. An off-street parking garage where the driver parks his own vehicle is called a _____ garage.

    A. self-parking   B. ramp
    C. commuter   D. mechanical

16. Off-street garages and lots where attendants park vehicles need adequate reservoir (storage) space at the entrance PRIMARILY to

    A. reduce customer waiting time when picking up cars
    B. reduce the number of attendants needed to park cars
    C. avoid spill-back of cars into the street system
    D. have extra space for parking cars when the garage fills up

17. Parking turnover is defined as the

    A. capacity of a parking lot or garage divided by the number of cars parked in it
    B. average number of times a parking space in a parking lot or garage is used during a given period of time
    C. number of empty spaces in a parking lot or garage
    D. number of space hours used during a day in a parking lot or garage

18. One-half hour parking meters would BEST serve customers of a(n)

    A. supermarket   B. medical building
    C. bank   D. office building

19. An off-street parking facility at a shopping center is operating at its BEST efficiency when it is _____ full 19.____

   A. 100%   B. 85%   C. 75%   D. 50%

20. 20.____

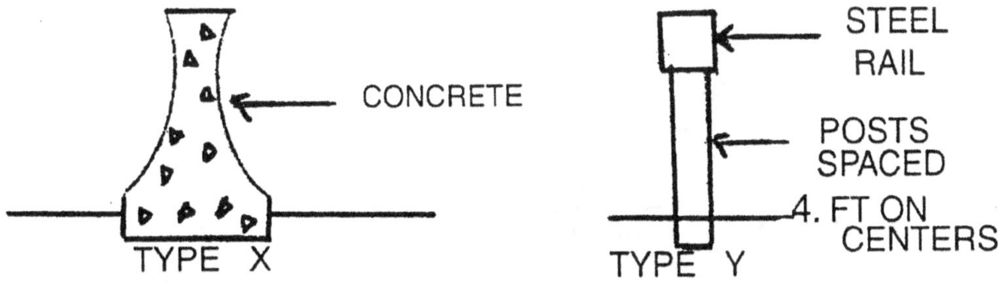

   Two types of barriers are shown above, Type X and Type Y. An *advantage* of Type X barrier over Type Y barrier is that Type X barrier _____ than Type Y.

   A. has a lower initial cost
   B. is easier to install
   C. requires less maintenance
   D. is more visible

21. A fatality is MOST likely to occur in a _____ accident. 21.____

   A. rear-end   B. right-angle
   C. side-swipe   D. head-on

22. Most accidents USUALLY occur 22.____

   A. during the morning rush hours
   B. at midday
   C. in the late afternoon and early evening
   D. between midnight and dawn

23. For the United States as a whole, studies have shown that alcohol was a contributing factor in _____ of the fatal accidents. 23.____

   A. 5%   B. 15%   C. 25%   D. 50%

24. The MAIN advantage of a red, yellow, and green light over a red and green light is that the red, yellow, and green light 24.____

   A. is less expensive
   B. is easier to install
   C. gives the driver warning of a change in signals from green to red
   D. gives the police officer firm evidence if he wants to issue a violation for passing a light

25. Dividing the total number of accidents occurring in one year on a roadway by the length of the roadway in miles will yield the 25._____

    A. fatality rate for the roadway
    B. accident rate per annual vehicle miles traveled
    C. accident exposure rate for the roadway
    D. accident rate per mile per year

KEY (CORRECT ANSWERS)

1.	D	11.	C
2.	A	12.	C
3.	C	13.	D
4.	D	14.	B
5.	C	15.	A
6.	C	16.	C
7.	B	17.	B
8.	B	18.	C
9.	A	19.	B
10.	D	20.	C

21. D
22. C
23. D
24. C
25. D

EXAMINATION SECTION
TEST 1

DIRECTIONS: Each question or incomplete statement is followed by several suggested answers or completions. Select the one that Best answers the question or completes the statement. *PRINT THE LETTER OF THE CORRECT ANSWER IN THE SPACE AT THE RIGHT.*

Questions 1-4.

DIRECTIONS: Answer Questions 1 to 4 based on the information given in the traffic volume table below.

TRAFFIC VOLUME COUNTS

Time (A.M.)	Main Street Northbound	Main Street Southbound	Cross Street Eastbound	Cross Street Westbound
7:00- 7:15	100	100	70	60
7:15- 7:30	110	100	80	70
7:30- 7:45	150	140	110	100
7:45- 8:00	170	160	140	130
8:00- 8:15	210	190	120	110
8:15- 8:30	180	170	90	80
8:30- 8:45	160	140	70	60
8:45- 9:00	150	160	70	50
9:00- 9:15	140	150	50	50
9:15- 9:30	130	120	40	20
9:30- 9:45	120	110	30	30
9:45-10:00	120	100	30	30

1. The hour during which traffic, moving in both directions on Main Street, reached its *peak* was

   A. 7:30 - 8:30
   B. 7:45 - 8:45
   C. 8:00 - 9:00
   D. 8:15 - 9:15

2. The hour during which traffic volume, moving in both directions on Cross Street, reached its *peak* was

   A. 7:30 - 8:30
   B. 7:45 - 8:45
   C. 8:00 - 9:00
   D. 8:15 - 9:15

3. The HIGHEST average hourly volume over the three-hour period 7:00 to 10:00 was recorded for

   A. Main Street northbound
   B. Main Street southbound
   C. Cross Street eastbound
   D. Cross Street westbound

4. The *peak* 15-minute traffic volume for all directions of travel occurred between

   A. 7:30 - 7:45
   B. 7:45 - 8:00
   C. 8:00 - 8:15
   D. 8:15 - 8:30

5. Which of the following statements relating to one-way streets is CORRECT?
   One-way streets

11

A. increase turning movement conflicts between vehicles
B. decrease street capacity
C. decrease accident hazards for pedestrians
D. make it impossible to time traffic signals to control speeds

Questions 6-11.

DIRECTIONS: Answer Questions 6 to 11 based on the information given in Figure 1 below.

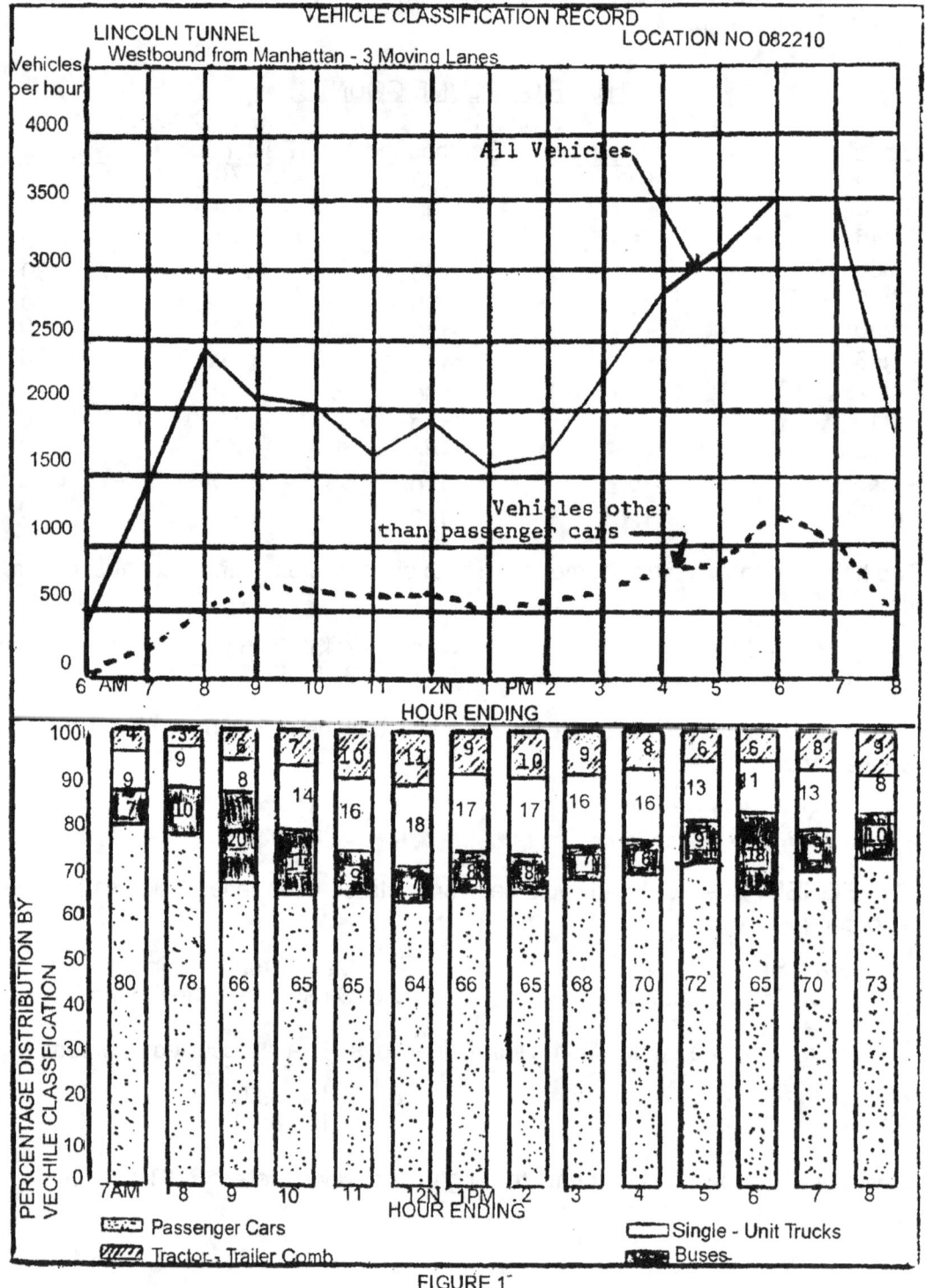

FIGURE 1

6. The total number of all vehicles traveling through the Lincoln Tunnel westbound from Manhattan between the hours of 6 A.M. and 12 Noon is *most nearly*

   A. 5,500   B. 7,500   C. 9,500   D. 11,500

7. The number of passenger cars recorded during the hour ending at 7 P.M. was *most nearly*

   A. 235   B. 1160   C. 2450   D. 3500

8. Excluding passenger cars, the AVERAGE number of vehicles per moving lane recorded during the peak hour was *most nearly*

   A. 420   B. 1180   C. 1250   D. 3550

9. The percentage of buses recorded between 6 A.M. and 8 P.M. ranged between

   A. 3% and 11%
   B. 8% and 18%
   C. 6% and 20%
   D. 64% and 80%

10. During the study period, the percentage of single unit trucks *exceeded* the percentage of buses for _____ hours.

    A. 4   B. 5   C. 9   D. 10

11. For all vehicles recorded, the recorded traffic volume during the morning peak hour was *most nearly* _____ of the volume during the evening peak hour.

    A. 40%   B. 50%   C. 60%   D. 70%

12. In urban areas, traffic volume is usually LOWEST during the month of

    A. January   B. March   C. August   D. October

13. In urban shopping areas, the *peak* traffic activity USUALLY occurs during

    A. Monday afternoon and Friday night
    B. Friday night and Saturday afternoon
    C. Thursday night and Saturday afternoon
    D. Monday night and Friday night

14. In the metric system, the unit that is closest to a mile is a

    A. centimeter
    B. liter
    C. millimeter
    D. kilometer

Questions 15-16.

DIRECTIONS: Questions 15 and 16 refer to the diagram at the top of the following Page 4.

15. Vehicle X in the diagram is heading in which direction?

    A. Southeast
    B. Southwest
    C. Northeast
    D. Northwest

16. If Vehicle X in the diagram makes a right turn at the intersection, it will be headed

    A. southeast
    B. southwest
    C. northeast
    D. northwest

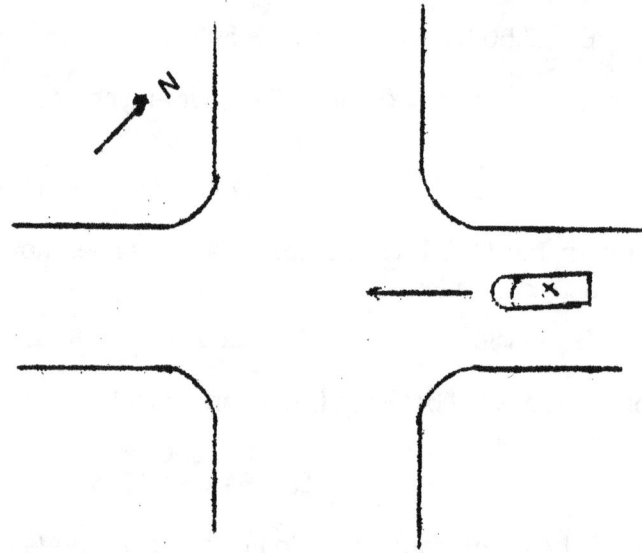

17. The one of the following that is NOT a function of channelization is

    A. control the angle of conflict
    B. favor certain turning movements
    C. protect pedestrians
    D. increase the pavement area within an intersection

17.____

18. The time of display of the yellow signal indication following the green signal indication is called the

    A. clearance interval
    B. time cycle
    C. traffic phase
    D. interval sequence

18.____

19. A lane constructed for the purpose of allowing vehicles entering a highway to increase speed to a rate that is safe for merging with through traffic is called a(n) _____ lane.

    A. auxiliary
    B. through
    C. acceleration
    D. deceleration

19.____

20. A traffic volume count which records the number and types of vehicles passing a given point is called a _____ count.

    A. rate-of-flow
    B. capacity
    C. classification
    D. roadway

20.____

21. On highways, the MAIN purpose served by barriers between traffic going in opposite directions is to

    A. stop cars if they get out of lane
    B. minimize the glare from oncoming cars
    C. prevent cars from overturning if they have blowouts
    D. prevent head-on accidents

21.____

22. Control count stations are USUALLY used to

    A. establish seasonal and daily traffic volume characteristics
    B. make short manual traffic counts
    C. classify traffic
    D. count traffic on weekends only

23. The MAIN purpose of off-center traffic lanes is to

    A. protect slow-moving traffic from the hazards of fast-moving traffic
    B. permit the use of special traffic control
    C. provide additional capacity in one direction of travel
    D. provide a slow-down area for disabled vehicles

24. Reserved transit lanes are used to

    A. make sure buses stop at the curb
    B. reduce bus and passenger car accidents
    C. decrease transit travel times by reducing friction between buses and other vehicles
    D. make it easier for people to get on and off buses

25. The slope or grade between points X and Y shown in the diagram below is

    A. 4%   B. 10%   C. 25%   D. 50%

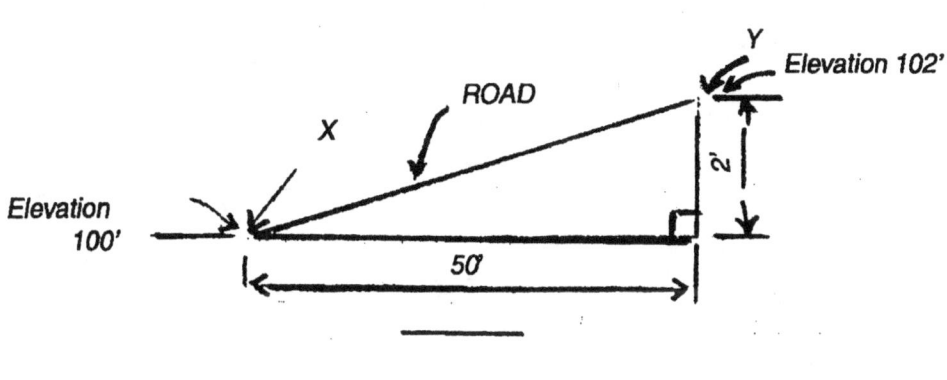

KEY (CORRECT ANSWERS)

1. B
2. A
3. A
4. C
5. C

6. D
7. C
8. A
9. C
10. C

11. D
12. A
13. B
14. D
15. B

16. D
17. D
18. A
19. C
20. C

21. D
22. A
23. C
24. C
25. A

TEST 2

DIRECTIONS: Each question or incomplete statement is followed by several suggested answers or completions. Select the one that BEST answers the question or completes the statement. *PRINT THE LETTER OF THE CORRECT ANSWER IN THE SPACE AT THE RIGHT.*

1. In the city, when parking is not otherwise restricted, commercial vehicles can park   1.____

   A. up to a maximum of one hour
   B. up to a maximum of three hours
   C. up to a maximum of eight hours
   D. without a time limitation

2. In the city, with respect to loading an parking, commercial vehicles are allowed to   2.____

   A. load or unload merchandise expeditiously in a no-standing zone
   B. park for one hour in a no-parking zone
   C. load or unload merchandise expeditiously in a no-parking zone
   D. park for one hour in a no-standing zone

3. On the Federal national highway system, highways ending in an even number run   3.____

   A. in the east-west direction
   B. both east-west or north-south
   C. in the north-south direction
   D. around cities and not through them

4. The *current* maximum allowed speed limit on Federal interstate highways is _____ miles per hour.   4.____

   A. 50   B. 55   C. 60   D. 65

5. In the city, when a vehicle is too long for a single parking meter space, the vehicle may   5.____

   A. not be parked in the parking meter area
   B. be parked using more than one space but a coin must be deposited in the meter designated for each space occupied
   C. be parked using more than one space and a coin must be deposited only in the forward parking meter
   D. be parked using more than one space and a coin must be deposited only in the rear parking meter

6. In the city, some signs indicate that stopping, standing, or parking regulations are in effect every day except Sundays. Where this sign is used, stopping, standing, or parking regulations would apply on   6.____

   A. Washington's Birthday   B. Brooklyn Day
   C. Columbus Day   D. Election Day

7. In the city, unless signs are posted indicating specific hours during which play street regulations are in effect, such regulations are in effect on designated streets FROM   7.____

   A. 7 A.M. until 4 P.M.
   B. 8 A.M. until 1/2 hour before sunset

17

C. 8 A.M. to 1/2 hour after sunset
D. 8 A.M. to 8 P.M.

8. When preparing to make a turn while driving a vehicle on a roadway, a driver should signal his intention to turn AT LEAST _____ feet in advance of the turn.

   A. 50   B. 100   C. 150   D. 200

9. Unless otherwise permitted or prohibited by posted signs, the MAXIMUM continuous period during which a vehicle may be parked on any roadway in the city is hours.

   A. 8   B. 12   C. 24   D. 48

10. In the city, commercial vehicles may angle stand or angle park in

    A. any area where no parking signs are installed, provided the street is wide enough to allow the vehicle to park at an angle
    B. on any one-way street where standing is not prohibited, provided the street is wide enough to allow the vehicle to park at an angle
    C. on a two-way street in areas authorized by signs, provided that the vehicle shall not occupy more than a parking lane plus one moving lane
    D. on a two-way street in areas authorized by signs, provided that the vehicles shall not extend more than 10 feet from the curb

11. Which of the following is MOST restrictive to drivers of passenger cars?

    A. Regulations relating to parking in front of fire hydrants
    B. No parking regulations
    C. No standing regulations
    D. No stopping regulations

12. The MAXIMUM permitted speed limit in the city, unless signs indicate otherwise, is _____ mph.

    A. 25   B. 30   C. 35   D. 40

13. With regard to right-of-way at an intersection that is NOT controlled by a traffic control device, the one of the following statements that is CORRECT is

    A. the car on your right has the right-of-way
    B. the car on your left has the right-of-way
    C. a car preparing to enter the intersection has the right-of-way over a car in the intersection
    D. a car turning left has the right-of-way over a vehicle going straight ahead

14. At an intersection controlled by traffic signals, a red arrow pointing to the right means that a right turn may

    A. be made after coming to a full stop
    B. be made providing the driver yields the right-of-way to all other vehicles and pedestrians
    C. not be made during the period that the red arrow is illuminated
    D. be made only if there is another indication showing a round green signal light

15. A flashing red traffic signal has the SAME meaning as a

    A. stop sign
    B. yield sign
    C. flashing yellow traffic signal
    D. hazardous intersection warning sign

16. Traffic signals are MOST frequently installed to reduce _____ collision accidents.

    A. right-angle   B. rear-end
    C. side-swipe   D. head-on

17. The CORRECT color combination for warning signs is

    A. yellow lettering or symbols on a black background
    B. white lettering or symbols on a red background
    C. black lettering or symbols on a yellow background
    D. black lettering or symbols on a white background

18. A PROGRESSIVELY timed traffic signal system will

    A. turn all the signals red or green at the same time
    B. usually increase the number of rear-end accidents but reduce the number of right-angle accidents
    C. make it more hazardous for pedestrians to cross at the signalized intersections
    D. decrease the number of stops traffic is required to make

19. The EFFECT of traffic signals on accidents is that traffic signals

    A. always decrease accidents
    B. sometimes increase accidents
    C. never increase accidents
    D. have no real effect on accidents

20. With respect to traffic devices, which of the following situations should receive the LOWEST priority in terms of repair or replacement?

    A. Inoperative or malfunctioning traffic signals at an intersection
    B. Missing "No Standing - Rush Hour" regulation signs
    C. Missing "Yield" signs controlling the intersection of a minor street with a major street
    D. Inoperative parking meters along one block in a retail shopping area

21. Of the following, the BEST reason why a stop sign would be used instead of a yield sign to control traffic at an intersection is

    A. there are a larger number of rear-end accidents on the street being controlled
    B. the street being controlled is less than 36 feet wide
    C. visibility is limited at the intersection
    D. the approaches to the intersection are offset to each other

22. The USUAL color combination used on interstate signs is _____ lettering and symbols on a _____ background.

    A. white; green   B. green; white
    C. white; black   D. black; white

23. The geometrical shape of a railroad crossing sign is that of a(n) 23.___

    A. octagon   B. circle   C. rectangle   D. triangle

24. The STANDARD pedestrian walking speed used in timing pedestrian signals is _____ per second. 24.___

    A. 1 foot   B. 4 feet   C. 8 feet   D. 12 feet

25. A driver approaching an intersection where a sign authorizes a right turn on a red traffic signal indication may make such a turn AND 25.___

    A. has the right-of-way over all vehicles in the intersection
    B. must yield right-of-way to all vehicles and pedestrians within the intersection
    C. must yield right-of-way only to vehicles and pedestrians on the cross street
    D. has the right-of-way over other turning vehicles

KEY (CORRECT ANSWERS)

1. B		11. D	
2. C		12. B	
3. A		13. A	
4. D		14. C	
5. C		15. A	
6. B		16. A	
7. C		17. C	
8. B		18. D	
9. C		19. B	
10. C		20. D	

21. C
22. A
23. B
24. B
25. B

EXAMINATION SECTION
TEST 1

DIRECTIONS: Each question or incomplete statement is followed by several suggested answers or completions. Select the one that BEST answers the question or completes the statement. *PRINT THE LETTER OF THE CORRECT ANSWER IN THE SPACE AT THE RIGHT.*

1. A traffic sign states that parking is permitted on Sundays and Holidays. According to the traffic regulations of the city, the holiday on which parking is NOT permitted in the area covered by the sign is

    A. New Year's Day   B. Memorial Day
    C. Thanksgiving Day   D. Lincoln's Birthday

2. An intrastate bus is a bus that runs

    A. only in one state
    B. in 2 states only
    C. between the United States and Canada
    D. between any states in the Union

3. According to the traffic regulations of the Department of Traffic, a pedestrian facing a red signal at an intersection

    A. has the right of way over automobiles having a green signal
    B. has the right of way over trucks having a green signal
    C. may not enter the intersection facing the red signal
    D. may enter the intersection, facing the red signal, if he can do so safely without interfering with traffic

4. This sentence was taken from the traffic regulations of the City Department of Traffic with respect to yield signs:
    Proceeding past such sign with resultant collision or other impedance or interference with traffic on the intersecting street shall be deemed prima facie in violation of this regulation. The words prima facie mean MOST NEARLY

    A. probably   B. possibly or likely
    C. literally or completely   D. guilty

5. Where signs on city streets do not indicate otherwise, the MAXIMUM speed limit in the city is, in miles per hour,

    A. 15   B. 20   C. 25   D. 30

6. Making a U-turn in the city is NOT permissible on any

    A. street
    B. street in a residential district
    C. street in a business district
    D. 2-way street

7. A person stops his car in front of a hydrant and remains in the car. According to the traffic regulations of the City Department of Traffic,

A. this is illegal if he is within 15 feet of the hydrant
B. it is legal
C. he does not have to move if so ordered by a policeman
D. he may remain there provided he is far enough away from the hydrant so as not to interfere with hose lines

8. Taxicabs are

   A. not permitted to cruise
   B. permitted to cruise in residential areas only
   C. permitted to cruise in business areas only
   D. permitted to cruise in all boroughs except Manhattan

9. Of the following, the one that is the MAIN cause of fatal accidents is

   A. direction signals not working
   B. windshield wipers not working
   C. improper alignment of the wheels
   D. defective brakes

10. The capacity of an approach to an intersection is prinarily dependent upon

    A. slope of through band
    B. cycle length
    C. offsets
    D. through band width

11. To handle heavy traffic movements which tend to cause congestion at an intersection, it is often necessary to

    A. use a standard 3-color (RAG) traffic control signal on all four corners
    B. add arrow indications to traffic signals permitting movements in a certain direction when other traffic is halted
    C. use 2-color instead of 3-color traffic signals
    D. install a flasher caution signal facing the direction of heavy traffic flow

12. Elm Street and Oak Street are one-way streets that intersect.

    A. Cars may turn either right from both streets or left from both streets depending on the direction of travel.
    B. If cars may turn right into one street, they may not turn right into the other.
    C. Only right turns are permitted in both streets.
    D. Only left turns are permitted in both streets.

13. Of the following intersections where one street dead ends into another, the one that is SAFEST is

    A. [diagram showing T-intersection at 70°]
    B. [diagram showing T-intersection at 60°]

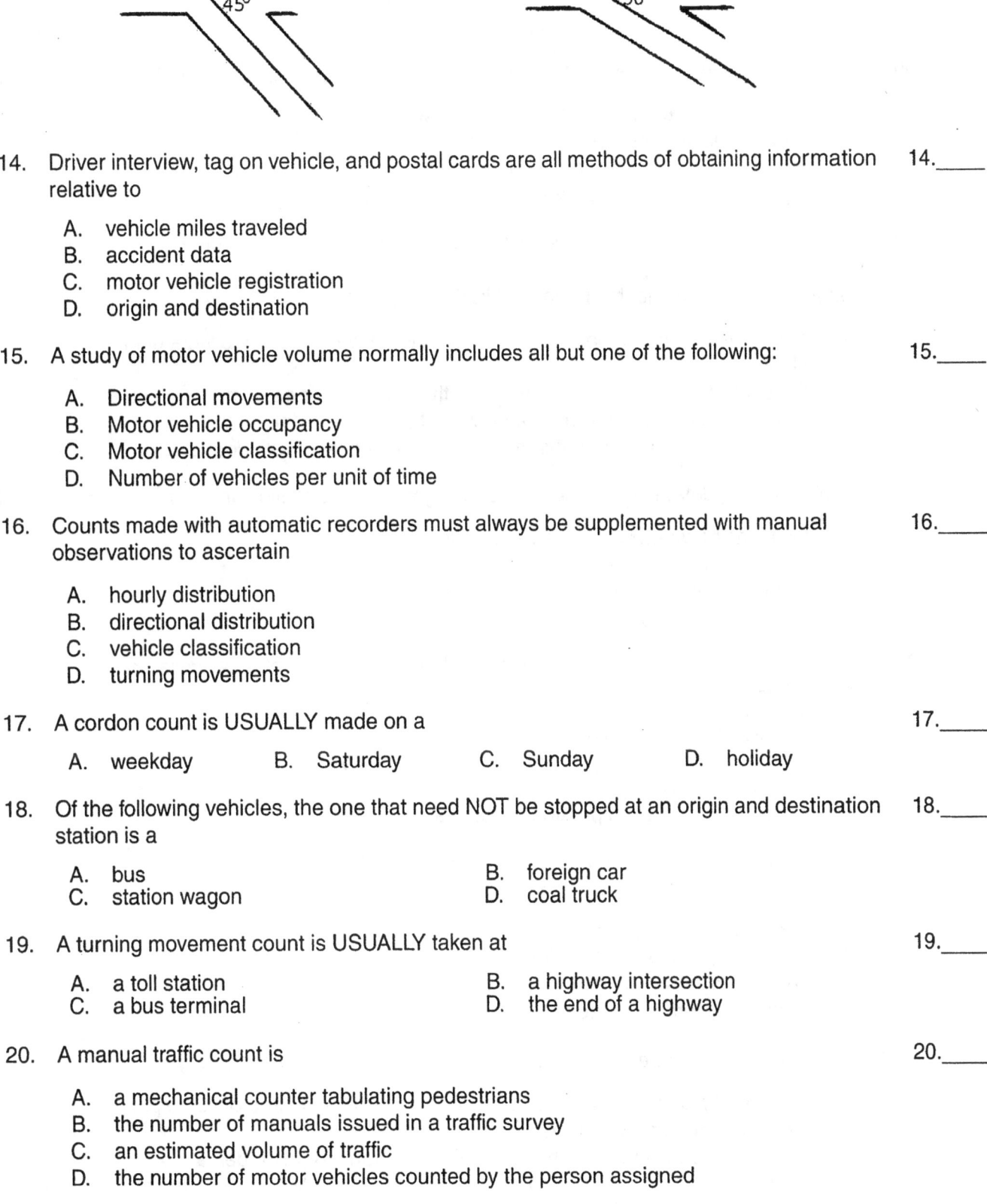

14. Driver interview, tag on vehicle, and postal cards are all methods of obtaining information relative to 14.____

    A. vehicle miles traveled
    B. accident data
    C. motor vehicle registration
    D. origin and destination

15. A study of motor vehicle volume normally includes all but one of the following: 15.____

    A. Directional movements
    B. Motor vehicle occupancy
    C. Motor vehicle classification
    D. Number of vehicles per unit of time

16. Counts made with automatic recorders must always be supplemented with manual observations to ascertain 16.____

    A. hourly distribution
    B. directional distribution
    C. vehicle classification
    D. turning movements

17. A cordon count is USUALLY made on a 17.____

    A. weekday   B. Saturday   C. Sunday   D. holiday

18. Of the following vehicles, the one that need NOT be stopped at an origin and destination station is a 18.____

    A. bus   B. foreign car
    C. station wagon   D. coal truck

19. A turning movement count is USUALLY taken at 19.____

    A. a toll station   B. a highway intersection
    C. a bus terminal   D. the end of a highway

20. A manual traffic count is 20.____

    A. a mechanical counter tabulating pedestrians
    B. the number of manuals issued in a traffic survey
    C. an estimated volume of traffic
    D. the number of motor vehicles counted by the person assigned

21. Traffic counts that are made within the city limits are _____ counts.

    A. rural
    B. suburban
    C. urban
    D. sample

22. When questioning a driver in a traffic survey, the interviewer should

    A. explain briefly the reason for the interview
    B. insist on having his questions answered
    C. get the signature of the person interviewed
    D. report the person interviewed, if he did not cooperate

23. In gathering data for a traffic survey, it was decided to use only the period from 6:00 A.M. to 10:00 P.M.
    The reason for choosing this period is MOST likely that

    A. employee morale would drop if the inspectors were required to work during the night
    B. the public would not cooperate during the late night or early morning hours
    C. it is inconsiderate to disturb the public in the middle of the night
    D. the information obtained at that time would be considered adequate

24. Of the following data, the one that is MOST significant in a traffic survey is the

    A. locations between which the car travels
    B. number of cars in the driver's family
    C. number of drivers operating the car
    D. average annual mileage of the car

25. The MAIN purpose for making a motor vehicle volume survey of a particular route is to provide basic data for determining

    A. the extent of group riding
    B. whether prevailing speeds are too fast for conditions
    C. a plan of traffic control
    D. where and how much parking space may be needed

26. Of the following studies, the one which is LEAST related and would probably NOT be included in making a traffic safety survey is

    A. street and off-street parking
    B. driver observance of stop signs
    C. pedestrian observance of traffic signals
    D. accident records and facts

27. Of the following, the one which would NOT usually require a traffic survey is

    A. revision of parking time limits to assure most efficient usage of curb space
    B. creation of off-street parking facilities
    C. important trends in traffic characteristics and transportation demands
    D. complaints from residents in a particular area on the disturbance caused by heavy traffic moving through that area

28. A *spot-map* is a graphic method which is used to

   A. show types of traffic signals located at the main intersections in a community
   B. analyze the distribution of accidents within a community area
   C. arrive at reasonable accident rates
   D. show grades, width, roadway surface, and merging traffic streams in a community

29. A survey was made for the purposes of installing traffic control signals at a certain intersection of a main street and cross street in a certain area. The survey shows that although traffic is relatively heavy during the day, it becomes very light at night.
   In such a situation, it would be MOST desirable to

   A. continue the full sequence of indications as in the daytime
   B. continue operation of the signals, but lengthen the cycle of intervals
   C. completely extinguish the signals leaving the intersection uncontrolled
   D. extinguish the signals but provide a flasher mechanism on the controller

30. If the capacity of an approach to an intersection is 3600 vehicles per hour of green and the go phase on this approach is 40 seconds out of a 60-second cycle, the equivalent volume is _____ vehicles per hour.

   A. 2400   B. 3600   C. 5400   D. 2000

31. If a section of a highway 10 miles long carries an annual daily traffic of 5,000 vehicles and there are two deaths in a year, the death rate is

   A. 2.0 deaths per 5,000 vehicles
   B. 11.0 deaths per 100 million vehicle miles
   C. 11.0 deaths per million vehicle miles
   D. 2.0 deaths per 50,000 vehicle miles

32. If the difference in elevation between two intersections 300 feet apart is 6 feet, the grade along the street is

   A. 2%   B. 2   C. 0.002   D. 6%

33. If on a highway a car passes a given point every 5 seconds, the number of cars per hour passing the given point on the highway is

   A. 360   B. 480   C. 600   D. 720

34. The cost of concrete paving for a strip of driveway 50 feet long, 10 feet wide, and 6 inches deep, if concrete in place costs $30 per cubic yard, is, in dollars, MOST NEARLY
   (27 cubic feet = 1 cubic yard)

   A. 278   B. 318   C. 329   D. 380

Questions 35-38.

DIRECTIONS: Questions 35 through 38 relate to the sketch below.

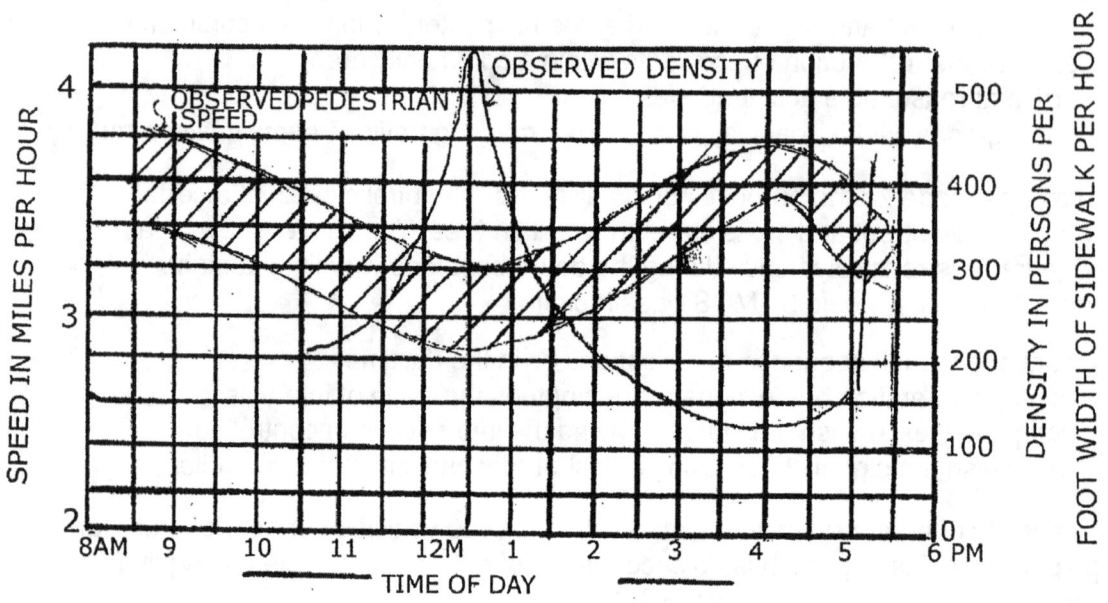

35. Assuming a 10' wide sidewalk, the number of people that would pass the given point at 12:00 M in 10 minutes is MOST NEARLY

    A. 580   B. 680   C. 780   D. 880

36. At 10:00 A.M., you could expect a person to be walking at a speed

    A. of 3 miles per hour
    B. between 300 and 420 feet per hour
    C. between 3.2 and 3.65 miles per hour
    D. of 4.5 feet per second

37. The highest average number of people using the sidewalk will USUALLY occur at

    A. 9 A.M.   B. 12:30 P.M.   C. 4 P.M.   D. 5 P.M.

38. Of the following statements relating to the diagram, the one that is MOST NEARLY CORRECT is

    A. the minimum walking speed observed is 2 miles per hour
    B. data for the survey was taken continuously for 24 hours
    C. as the number of people using the sidewalk increases, the speed at which they walk decreases
    D. the minimum observed density is 300 people per hour per foot width of sidewalk

39. A vehicle moving at 30 miles per hour is moving at a speed, in feet per second, MOST NEARLY

    A. 30   B. 44   C. 52   D. 60

40. A street map is to a scale 1 inch equals 600 feet. A distance of 1/2 inch on the drawing represents a distance on the ground, in feet, MOST NEARLY

    A. 300   B. 600   C. 900   D. 1,200

Questions 41-42.

DIRECTIONS: Questions 41 and 42 refer to the sketches below.

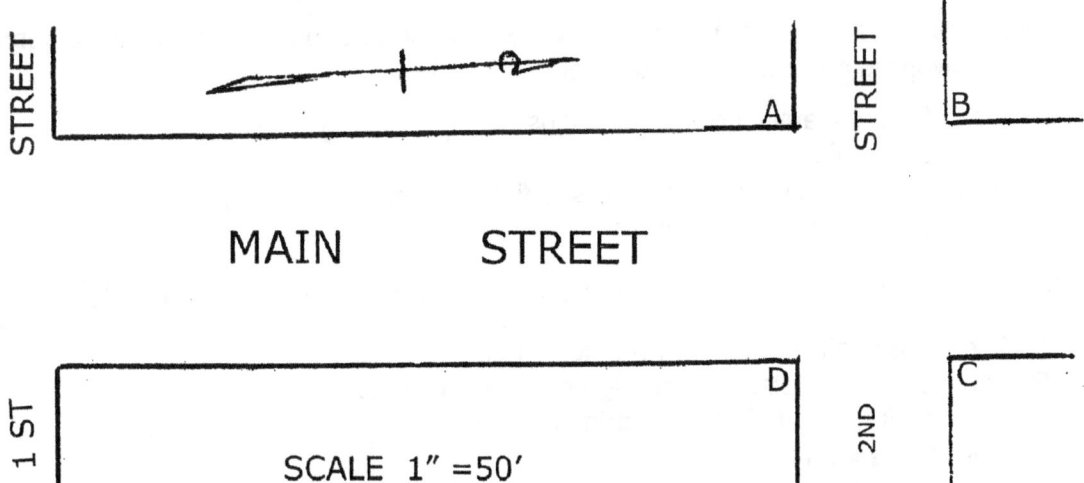

41. The length of block from 1st Street to 2nd Street is MOST NEARLY   41.____

    A. 150'   B. 250'   C. 350'   D. 450'

42. The northeast corner of Main and 2nd is   42.____

    A. A   B. B   C. C   D. D

43. The sketch shown at the right shows a right triangular island at the intersection of three streets on which is installed traffic signals A and B. Traffic conditions have increased and require than an additional traffic light be installed at point C. Electric power for signal C is to be taken from the junction box located at the base of post A and extended to C as shown by the broken line. With the distances given as shown, the length of conduit, in feet, required to extend power from A to C is MOST NEARLY   43.____

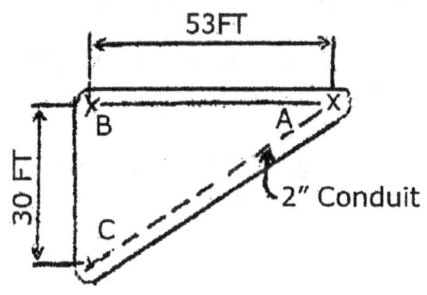

    A. 44   B. 60   C. 83   D. 75

44. The volume of traffic at a certain location increased frori 1,000 to 1,500 vehicles per hour. The percentage increase of traffic is MOST NEARLY   44.____

    A. 33%   B. 50%   C. 60%   D. 40%

45. A collision diagram would MOST likely NOT show   45.____

    A. direction of movement of each vehicle or pedestrian involved
    B. distance of the accident to the nearest building line
    C. date and hour of the accident
    D. weather and road conditions

46. A graphical representation of the detailed nature of accidents occurring at a location is known as a

    A. collision diagram
    B. condition diagram
    C. accident summary
    D. accident spot map

47. Which one of the following remedies is MOST appropriate to eliminate high accident frequency involving collisions with fixed objects?

    A. Installation of advance warning signs
    B. Reroute traffic
    C. Application of paint and reflectors to fixed object
    D. Installation of center dividing strip

48. One of the reasons for making a study of driver observance of stop signs is to study the

    A. need for retaining or removing stop signs
    B. desirability of replacing stop sign with a police officer
    C. desirability of installing pedestrian crosswalk lines
    D. need for speed zoning

49. Which one of the following remedies is MOST appropriate to eliminate high accident frequency involving pedestrian-vehicular collisions at intersections?

    A. Installation of turning guide lines
    B. Installation of painted pavement lane lines
    C. Installation of pedestrian cross-walk lines
    D. Removal of view obstruction

50. The driver of a vehicle approaching a yield sign is required to

    A. proceed without changing speed
    B. slow down if there is a vehicle in the intersection
    C. stop
    D. slow down and proceed with caution

KEY (CORRECT ANSWERS)

1. D	11. B	21. C	31. B	41. B
2. A	12. B	22. A	32. A	42. C
3. C	13. A	23. D	33. D	43. B
4. C	14. D	24. A	34. A	44. B
5. C	15. B	25. C	35. A	45. B
6. C	16. C	26. A	36. C	46. A
7. A	17. A	27. D	37. B	47. C
8. A	18. A	28. B	38. C	48. A
9. D	19. B	29. D	39. B	49. C
10. D	20. D	30. A	40. A	50. D

TEST 2

DIRECTIONS: Each question or incomplete statement is followed by several suggested answers or completions. Select the one that BEST answers the question or completes the statement. *PRINT THE LETTER OF THE CORRECT ANSWER IN THE SPACE AT THE RIGHT.*

1. No person shall stop, stand, or park a vehicle closer to a fire hydrant than   1.____

    A. 17'   B. 10'   C. 15'   D. 12'

2. When stopping is prohibited by signs or regulations and no conflict exists with other traffic, the driver of a vehicle is   2.____

    A. permitted to stop temporarily
    B. not permitted to stop
    C. permitted to stand
    D. permitted to park

3. Where there is a *No Parking* sign, a person may   3.____

    A. not stop his vehicle
    B. stop his vehicle to discharge passengers
    C. stop his vehicle and leave it unattended for a maximum of 10 minutes
    D. stop his vehicle and leave it unattended for a maximum of 5 minutes

4. Of the following, the MOST restrictive parking sign is   4.____

    A. no standing   B. no parking
    C. taxi stand   D. bus stop

5. A highway sign that is classified as a Guide sign is   5.____

    A. Stop   B. No Passing
    C. Narrow Road   D. North Bound

6. A highway sign that is classified as a Warning sign is   6.____

    A. No U Turn   B. Hill
    C. Speed Limit 50   D. Do Not Enter

7. A highway sign that is classified as a Regulatory sign is   7.____

    A. One Way   B. Men Working
    C. RR   D. Detour

8. A traffic device that has the same effect as a stop sign is a   8.____

    A. flashing yellow   B. flashing red
    C. yield sign   D. detour sign

9. A warrant for a certain type of traffic control device is a(n)   9.____

    A. official order to install the device
    B. application from a local community for the device
    C. reason for installing the device
    D. request to remove the device

29

10. Shapes of signs on state highways convey definite information. The sign to the right means
    A. steep hill - slow down
    B. come to a full stop
    C. you may proceed with caution
    D. approaching narrow bridge

11. Where flasher mechanisms must be installed at intersections of a main street and a cross street as a warning signal, it would be BEST to have flashing
    A. amber on the main street and flashing red on the cross street
    B. red on the main street and flashing amber on the cross street
    C. red on the main street only
    D. amber on the cross street only

12. The primary purpose of *progressive timing* of traffic control signals is to
    A. allow the largest volume of traffic flow at the safest speed along a particular route
    B. permit slow drivers to travel at an increased speed
    C. permit the largest volume of pedestrian traffic to cross safely at the same time
    D. reduce traveling speed so that motorists have vehicles under constant control

13. A hazard marker, for example, at the end of a dead-end street, would MOST likely be
    A. yellow background with black letters
    B. yellow background with red letters
    C. a reflector type marker
    D. a warning sign

14. Of the following, the BEST reason for having markings that are uniform in design, position, and application is that
    A. less skill is required to provide the markings
    B. they cost less when they are uniform
    C. there is no harm done in providing them even where there is no need
    D. they may be recognized and understood instantly

15. If numerous pedestrian accidents occur at a signalized intersection, a pertinent study to help evaluate the problem would be
    A. signal timing
    B. motor vehicle volume
    C. pedestrian observance of traffic signals
    D. driver observance of pedestrian right of way

16. Which one of the following types of fixed-time signal systems is MOST desirable? _____ system.
    A. Flexible progressive   B. Alternate
    C. Simple progressive   D. Simultaneous

17. Of the following statements relating to traffic actuated signals, the one that is CORRECT is   17._____

    A. it is especially useful at little used intersections
    B. the length of time the green light is on is not constant
    C. it can only be used at the intersection of one-way streets
    D. it can only be used at the intersection of two-way streets

18. An advantage of the three lens signal (red, yellow, and green) over the two lens signal (red and green) is that it   18._____

    A. enables cars within the intersection to clear
    B. allows pedestrians to cross the intersection safely
    C. may be operated as a traffic actuated signal
    D. may be used as a caution signal when not used as a stop and go signal

19. A fixed time signal is one by which traffic stops and goes   19._____

    A. for equal time periods
    B. according to a predetermined time schedule
    C. by manual control
    D. according to the volume of traffic

20. The proper installation of vehicle detectors is MOST important for a   20._____

    A. pedestrian push-button installation
    B. fixed time signal system
    C. traffic actuated signal
    D. progressive system

21. Of the following, the one that is NOT considered a disadvantage in the use of pavement markings is they   21._____

    A. may be obliterated by snow
    B. may not be clearly visible when wet
    C. must be used with other devices such as traffic signs or signals
    D. are subject to traffic wear

22. *It is often desirable to mark lines on the pavement to indicate the limits and the clearance of the overhang on turning streetcars.*
    This safety measure is NOT required in this city because   22._____

    A. there are no streetcars in this city
    B. city traffic is controlled by other suitable devices
    C. city traffic is not fast enough to require it
    D. streetcars in this city turn only at the depot and not in the streets

23. A yellow curb marking may be used at all but one of the following: 23._____

    A. A fire hydrant
    B. A bus stop
    C. A depressed curb leading to a loading platform
    D. Where parking is prohibited from 8 A.M. to 6 P.M.

24. Stop lines or limit lines are used to indicate

    A. parking space limits to prevent encroachment on a fire hydrant zone
    B. the marking of stalls where parking meters are used
    C. the point behind which vehicles must stop in compliance with a traffic signal
    D. where pedestrians are permitted to cross a street

25. An island, as applied to traffic control,

    A. provides a safe area for a traffic patrolman
    B. segregates pedestrians and vehicles
    C. provides a clear area for a bus stop
    D. establishes a barrier between opposite lanes of traffic

26. Of the following, the one which is NOT a method for providing channelization of traffic is by

    A. permanent islands or strips
    B. pavement markings
    C. use of stanchions
    D. mounting traffic signal at center of intersection

27. The PRIMARY purpose for marking the pavement of heavily traveled thoroughfares into lanes is to

    A. slow up traffic
    B. prevent accidents
    C. speed up traffic
    D. keep slow drivers on the right side of the road

28. When parking is not otherwise restricted in the city, no person shall park a commercial vehicle in excess of hours.

    A. 2   B. 4   C. 3   D. 6

29. A condition which need NOT be considered in making a general parking survey is

    A. reasons for parking at various locations
    B. street and roadway widths and surfaces
    C. average time vehicles remained at various locations
    D. sidewalk obstructions, such as lamp posts and fire posts

30. Concerning the purpose of parking meters, the statement which is NOT true is

    A. assist in reducing overtime parking at the curb
    B. increase parking turnover
    C. eliminate the need for off-street parking facilities
    D. facilitate enforcement of parking regulations

31. The MOST efficient layout of parking spaces in a large lot is to place the stalls _____ to the aisles.

    A. parallel   B. at right angles
    C. at a 30° angle   D. at a 60° angle

32. The time limits set by cities for parking on city streets during the daytime 32._____

    A. is considered strictly a policing problem
    B. is shorter in concentrated business areas
    C. will vary directly with the amount of traffic on the street
    D. is uniform for all sections of the city

33. Four parts of a survey report are listed below, not necessarily in their proper order: 33._____
    I. Body of report
    II. Synopsis of report
    III. Letter of transmittal
    IV. Conclusions

    Which one of the following represents the BEST sequence for inclusion of these parts in a report?

    A. III, IV, I, II   B. II, I, III, IV
    C. III, II, I, IV   D. I, III, IV, II

34. A traffic control inspector recommends that an illuminated advertising sign near a signal light be removed. 34._____
    The reason for this recommendation is MOST likely that

    A. a driver's attention may be attracted to the sign rather than the road
    B. the similarity of colors may cause confusion
    C. such signs mar the beauty of the roadside
    D. the sign encroaches upon public property

35. Of the following, the MOST important value of a good report is that it 35._____

    A. reflects credit upon the person who submitted the report
    B. provides good reference material
    C. expedites official business
    D. expresses the need for official action

36. The MOST important requirement in report writing is 36._____

    A. promptness in turning in reports
    B. length
    C. grammatical construction
    D. accuracy

37. You have discovered an error in your report submitted to the main office. 37._____
    You should

    A. wait until the error is discovered in the main office and then correct it
    B. go directly to the supervisor in the main office after working hours and ask him unofficially to correct the answer
    C. notify the main office immediately so that the error can be corrected if necessary
    D. do nothing, since it is possible that one error will have little effect on the total report

38. The use of *radar* by police as a means of apprehending motorists who exceed the speed limit has recently been challenged in court on the grounds that 38._____

    A. the motorists are not forewarned
    B. the speed limits have not been posted

C. the equipment does not give reliable results
D. there is no sworn evidence that a speed violation took place

39. Of the following, the one which is generally classified as a commercial vehicle is a   39.____

    A. station wagon
    B. chauffeur-driven passenger car
    C. taxicab
    D. truck

40. A divided arterial highway for through traffic with full or partial control of access is generally referred to as an   40.____

    A. expressway   B. parkway
    C. freeway   D. major street

41. Of the following, the MOST important advantage to be gained by converting a two-way north-south street to a one-way street is   41.____

    A. *decrease* the number of accidents
    B. *decrease* the need for bus service
    C. *increase* the average speed of traffic
    D. *increase* the turnover at curbs

42. Of the following, the BEST road for heavy traffic is   42.____

    A. two lane   B. three lane
    C. four lane undivided D. four lane divided

43. When weekend traffic differs greatly from weekday traffic,   43.____

    A. the average daily traffic figure is used in estimating weekend traffic
    B. weekend traffic counts should be made as well as weekday counts
    C. the traffic count for another road in the area should be used
    D. traffic counts should be made at different seasons of the year

44. Work is now going on to approximately double the car-carrying capacity of which one of the following?   44.____

    A. Car parkways   B. Bridges
    C. Tunnels   D. HOV lanes

45. The MOST recent major change in the specifications of the federally aided highway program is   45.____

    A. increasing the permissible grades or roads
    B. requirements for drainage
    C. lane width
    D. vertical clearance under bridges

46. A recent newspaper article reported that small cars are considered a danger to the federally aided highway program.   46.____
    Of the following, the one that may be considered as the reason for this danger is

A. they consume less gas providing less taxes for the highway program
B. the lanes of the new highways are too wide for these cars, disorganizing the traffic flow pattern
C. the two-car family is upsetting the estimates of traffic flow
D. foreign cars are hurting American business

47. Span-wire mountings of fixed traffic control signals is generally   47.____

    A. used in the city at heavily traveled intersections
    B. used in the city at intersections in isolated areas
    C. not used in the city
    D. used at locations where more than two streets intersect

48. A map depicting straight lines drawn from points of vehicle origin to points of vehicle destination is known as _____ map.   48.____

    A. desire line   B. traffic flow
    C. bar   D. pie

49. Brake reaction time for most people is APPROXIMATELY _____ seconds.   49.____

    A. 0.6   B. 2.0   C. 0.1   D. 1.4

50. Trucks should travel along prescribed truck routes if their overall length is equal to or exceeds   50.____

    A. 27'   B. 41'   C. 30'   D. 33'

KEY (CORRECT ANSWERS)

1. C	11. A	21. C	31. B	41. C
2. B	12. A	22. A	32. B	42. D
3. B	13. C	23. D	33. C	43. B
4. A	14. D	24. C	34. B	44. D
5. D	15. C	25. B	35. C	45. D
6. B	16. A	26. D	36. D	46. A
7. A	17. B	27. C	37. C	47. C
8. B	18. D	28. C	38. C	48. A
9. C	19. B	29. D	39. D	49. A
10. B	20. C	30. C	40. A	50. D

EXAMINATION SECTION
TEST 1

DIRECTIONS: Each question or incomplete statement is followed by several suggested answers or completions. Select the one that BEST answers the question or completes the statement. *PRINT THE LETTER OF THE CORRECT ANSWER IN THE SPACE AT THE RIGHT.*

Questions 1-5.

DIRECTIONS: Questions 1 through 5 are based on the map shown in the Memory Pages, which appear at the end of the test.

1. The map shown in the Memory Pages is a map of   1.____
   - A. Daneville
   - B. Danville
   - C. Deanville
   - D. Denville

2. On the other side of Broadway, Jones Street becomes   2.____
   - A. Allan Street
   - B. Central Avenue
   - C. Paul Street
   - D. Roger Street

3. The ONLY one of the following which goes diagonally rather than North and South or East and West is   3.____
   - A. Allan Terrace
   - B. Allan Street
   - C. Broadway
   - D. Central Avenue

4. In order to walk from Jones Street to Roger Street along Central Avenue, which of the following streets is it necessary to cross?   4.____
   - A. Allan Street
   - B. Allan Terrace
   - C. Park Street
   - D. Paul Street

5. If you were walking along Roger Street and wanted to get to the Park, it would be necessary to go   5.____
   - A. west
   - B. north
   - C. south
   - D. east

Questions 6-10.

DIRECTIONS: Questions 6 through 10 are based on the drawings of the two intersections in the Memory Pages, which appear at the end of the test.

6. A *Don't Walk* sign is shown at the intersection of   6.____
   - A. Howard Street and Pell Avenue
   - B. Morley Lane and Howard Street
   - C. Pell Avenue and Richard Avenue
   - D. Richard Avenue and Morley Lane

7. Which of the following signs is shown at Intersection No. 1?   7.____
   - A. School
   - B. Slow
   - C. Stop
   - D. Yield

8. What is the speed limit specified at Intersection No. 2?

   A. 25　　　　B. 30　　　　C. 35　　　　D. 40

9. Which two vehicles are pictured at Intersection No. 1? A(n)

   A. taxi and a private car
   B. truck and an ambulance
   C. ambulance and a private car
   D. ambulance and a taxi

10. Which two vehicles are pictured at Intersection No. 2? A(n)

    A. ambulance and a taxi
    B. private car and a taxi
    C. taxi and a truck
    D. truck and a private car

Questions 11-12.

DIRECTIONS: Questions 11 through 12 are based on the Memory Pages, which appear at the end of the test.

11. Which of the following license numbers is shown in the Memory Pages?

    A. BR7981　　　B. YFN863　　　C. TPN683　　　D. FR9781

12. The license plates shown in the Memory Pages are from which of the following states?

    A. New Jersey and North Carolina
    B. New Jersey and North Dakota
    C. New York and North Carolina
    D. New York and North Dakota

Questions 13-31.

DIRECTIONS: In answering Questions 13 through 31, assume that you are on duty. You are wearing a uniform that identifies you to the public, and you are equipped with a two-way radio (a walkie-talkie) that links you with headquarters for your area your *command station*.

13. There are a number of different bus routes that have corner stops near your intersection. Some buses follow the avenue; some follow the cross-street; some have special destinations. You are familiar with all the bus routes and stops. A pedestrian comes to you and asks, *Where can I get a bus?*
    Generally, the FIRST thing you should say to the pedestrian is

    A. Where do you want to go?
    B. On any corner.
    C. Please wait until I finish directing traffic.
    D. There's a bus coming right now -- just get on it.

14. Drivers and pedestrians often ask you for directions to different places in the city. Which of the following directions would be EASIEST for an out-of-town visitor to understand and follow?

    A. Right
    B. South
    C. Downtown
    D. Lower East Side

15. During the morning rush hour, the traffic lights on your corner suddenly stop working. The traffic lights on all the other corners that you can see are still working, however. Which of the following actions is MOST appropriate in this situation?

    A. Keep traffic moving on the same schedule as if the lights were working, by using the second hand of your watch to time the intervals.
    B. Return to your command station as rapidly as possible.
    C. Keep traffic moving as smoothly as possible in all directions, using your own judgment to prevent traffic in any direction from getting snarled or jammed.
    D. Slow all traffic until you hear from your command station.

16. It is the start of the morning rush hour, and you are directing traffic at an intersection where emergency street-repair work is blocking one westbound traffic lane and a pedestrian crosswalk. You are having trouble controlling both pedestrians and vehicles, and westbound traffic is getting backed up. You feel that the situation requires an additional agent for proper control.
    Of the following, which course of action should you take FIRST?

    A. Call the police
    B. Call your command station to explain the situation and ask if additional help is available
    C. Direct the repair crew to stop work until after rush hour
    D. Close off the street on which the repair work is being done

17. There is a sign on a pole at your intersection that reads *NO LEFT TURN*. You arrive on duty one day and notice that the sign has been so badly bent that drivers probably cannot read it.
    Which of the following actions should be taken?

    A. Allow left turns, but do not assume responsibility for reporting the bent sign
    B. Do not allow left turns, but do not assume responsibility for reporting the bent sign
    C. Allow left turns, and report the bent sign
    D. Do not allow left turns, and report the bent sign

18. A new building is going up near the intersection where you are directing traffic. The construction company has been given permission to place equipment on the four-lane north-south avenue but only in the outside northbound lane next to the curb. You see a large compressor being placed by the foreman of the construction site so that it blocks half of the inside northbound lane as well.
    Your FIRST action should be to

    A. ask the foreman to move the compressor so that it does not block the inside lane
    B. direct all northbound traffic into the inside southbound lane
    C. serve a summons for a parking violation
    D. call your supervisor and ask him to phone the construction company about the situation

19. A large empty carton fell off a truck as the truck turned the corner at your intersection. It was not possible to get the driver's attention, and the truck is now a block away. The carton is not heavy, but it is about three feet high and it is lying in a lane, although not blocking it completely.
You should

    A. run after the truck driver to tell him he has lost a carton
    B. move the carton out of the way of traffic
    C. direct traffic around the carton until the truck driver or the Sanitation Department removes it
    D. call your command station to report the situation

20. Traffic has been moving smoothly at your intersection when a driver stops in the middle of the intersection and asks you, *How do I get to the Staten Island ferry?* His car has an Oregon license plate.
Which of the following responses is MOST desirable?

    A. Wave him on in as friendly a manner as possible.
    B. Have him pull over to the curb, then walk over and give him directions.
    C. Tell him to inquire at a gas station.
    D. Stop traffic briefly while you make certain that the out-of-town visitor thoroughly understands your directions.

21. When you arrive on duty at your intersection, you see a man lying against the curb. On being questioned, he says he has been hit by a car and cannot get up, but his story is confused. He appears dirty and shabby.
What action should you take?

    A. Call your command station for assistance, asking for an ambulance.
    B. Test his rationality by asking him his name, address, and phone number.
    C. Ask a passerby to phone for an ambulance, so that responsibility for the decision can be shared.
    D. Ignore the man, since he is probably a drunken bum.

22. Assume that you are controlling traffic at an intersection. The streets are two-way streets with one lane in each direction, and the traffic is very heavy. You hear the siren of an emergency vehicle. You cannot see the vehicle yet, and you are not sure which street it is on, but it seems to be coming closer.
Which of the following actions is MOST appropriate?

    A. Halt all traffic at the intersection until the vehicle goes through.
    B. Keep all traffic restricted to just one lane on each street until the emergency vehicle has passed.
    C. Keep traffic moving on one street and halt all traffic on the cross-street.
    D. Keep all traffic moving as quickly and smoothly as possible.

23. A taxi and a car have just collided, and a passenger in the taxi is unconscious and bleeding.
What should you do FIRST?

    A. Serve summonses on both drivers.
    B. Get the names and addresses of witnesses.

C. Give first aid to the passenger, if you can, and call for an ambulance.
D. Keep directing traffic, but notify your command station that there has been a collision.

24. A young white man with brown, curly hair drove a green Chevrolet four-door sedan westbound on 42nd Street through your intersection at 42nd Street and Fifth Avenue. The green light was in his favor, but westbound traffic was backed up on 42nd Street to Fifth Avenue. You clearly motioned him to stop. You serve a summons, and he says,
The light was in my favor. I'm going to fight this summons.
You make the following notes to be sure that you will remember the important details of the incident:
  Driver's name is James C. Martin. Green Chevrolet 4-door sedan is registered in his name, plate no. 000-ZYZ. Went through intersection of 42nd Street and Fifth, headed west on 42nd, against hand signal. Date 6/1/09, time 11:35 A.M.
Which of the following NOT included in your notes might be important if you ever have to give an official explanation of the incident?

A. He can be recognized because he is white with curly, brown hair.
B. Traffic was backed up on 42nd Street to the intersection.
C. I had signaled him to stop.
D. The car was registered in his name as owner.

25. You are directing traffic at an intersection near a tunnel exit. Halfway down the block in the direction of the tunnel, a truck becomes disabled. Traffic begins to back up rapidly behind the disabled vehicle.
Of the following, which is the BEST thing for you to do?

A. Call your command station to send a supervisor to the scene to evaluate the situation.
B. Assume that the officers on duty at the tunnel will take care of the problem.
C. Serve a summons on the truck driver for blocking traffic.
D. Call your command station to request a tow truck as well as extra traffic control help.

26. You have to give a police officer the important facts about an accident you have witnessed, and you will also be expected to testify as a witness at a hearing.
You provide him with the following notes:
May 12, 2009, 11:15 A.M., southwest corner of 34th Street and Second Avenue. The driver of the car was John M. Smith. The pedestrian was Betty L. Jones. The pedestrian was crossing from the southwest to the southeast corner of 34th Street when the car turned south on Second Avenue from 34th Street.
Which of the following questions is NOT answered by your notes?

A. Who was involved in the accident?
B. Where was the accident?
C. When was the accident?
D. What was the accident?

27. Your regular supervisor is on leave of absence, and a temporary supervisor has just taken over. The temporary supervisor tells you to carry out a certain procedure in a different way from the way you were doing it before. You think that the old way was better, and you have some good reasons to back up your opinion.
What should you do?

    A. Continue to carry out the procedure in the old way, but do not let your temporary supervisor know what you are doing.
    B. Continue to carry out the procedure in the old way, and be prepared to give your reasons to your temporary supervisor if you are questioned.
    C. Explain the old procedure to the temporary supervisor, present reasons for retaining the old method, and ask the temporary supervisor if he still wants you to change the procedure.
    D. Follow the new method, but plan to make a complaint when your regular supervisor gets back.

28. A new agent has been assigned to duty with you at an intersection where you have been directing traffic for several months. He allows a taxidriver to make an illegal turn.
What should you do in this situation?

    A. Serve a summons on the taxidriver.
    B. Report the new agent to your supervisor at the end of your tour.
    C. Explain to the new agent, as soon as you can, that the turn was illegal and that he should not allow such turns in the future.
    D. Jot the error down on a list and plan to take it up with the new agent at the end of the day, along with all the other errors that you can spot in his behavior.

29. You had a bad case of flu for several days. This is your first day back on duty, but after an hour you begin to feel very dizzy and weak. You are alone at your intersection.
What should you do?

    A. Go home to avoid endangering yourself and others, and call your command station from home to inform them that you are again on sick leave.
    B. Leave your post for just a few minutes for a rest and a cup of coffee, hoping that this will give you the necessary strength to do your duty.
    C. Try to carry on as long as possible, directing traffic from the curb so that you aren't in danger because of your slow reactions.
    D. Call for assistance and plan to go off duty, since your job is one where your condition endangers yourself and others.

30. It is the evening rush hour. Traffic is moving very slowly, and drivers are short-tempered. One driver leans out of his car window as he passes you and curses you, although you have done nothing to deserve such nasty remarks.
What should you do about this driver?

    A. Order him to pull over to the curb, and give him a summons.
    B. Stop him and tell him in no uncertain terms that his abuse of a public servant shows his lack of good citizenship.
    C. Shout back at him that you are as annoyed by traffic as he is.
    D. Ignore him and keep your attention on the movement of traffic.

31. Assume that you halt a motorist for driving past a Stop sign without stopping. He tells you that he knew he was supposed to stop, but that there was no traffic going in any direction. You know that this is true. However, you have been told to follow a policy of strict enforcement.
The MOST appropriate action for you to take in this situation is to

   A. let him go with a stern warning
   B. issue a summons
   C. make him back up and repeat the correct procedure
   D. ignore the offense and save your energies for real traffic violators

32. Of the following, the MOST important purpose of traffic laws and rules is to

   A. reduce the speed of traffic
   B. prevent traffic accidents
   C. establish consistent traffic patterns
   D. control the volume and destination of traffic

33. The laws of most states in the United States require formal examination of applicants before obtaining a driver's license.
Of the following, the MOST basic reason for these examinations is to

   A. test the eyesight of potential drivers
   B. collect fees for licensing drivers
   C. make it easier to register a motor vehicle
   D. insure that the driver is able to control his vehicle

34. Traffic accidents are usually the result of one or more violations of traffic laws.
Of the following, it can most reasonably be inferred from this statement that the BEST way to reduce traffic accidents is to

   A. reduce the number of high-powered vehicles
   B. build safer and more efficient highways
   C. get more motorists to obey the traffic laws
   D. increase the safety features of motor vehicles

35. A traffic regulation states that *No person shall back a vehicle into an intersection or over a crosswalk and shall not in any event or at any place back a vehicle unless such movement can be made in safety*
According to this regulation,

   A. an agent is right in issuing a summons to any driver he sees backing up on a street
   B. it is permissible for a driver to back up over a crosswalk if there is no one behind him
   C. a driver may back up in the middle of a block if there are no cars coming and if he is careful
   D. there is no reason why a driver should ever have to back up under city driving conditions

36. A traffic regulation says, *No driver shall enter an intersection unless there is sufficient unobstructed space beyond the intersection to accommodate the vehicle he is operating, notwithstanding any traffic control signal indication to the contrary.*
    This regulation means that a driver should

    A. not go through an intersection if there are no parking spaces available in the next block
    B. not enter an intersection when the traffic light is red
    C. not enter an intersection if traffic ahead of him is so badly backed up that he would not be able to go ahead and would block the intersection
    D. ignore traffic signals completely whenever there are obstructions in the road ahead of him

37. A traffic regulation concerning traffic signals reads as follows: *Flashing DON'T WALK - Pedestrians facing such signal are warned that there is insufficient time to cross the roadway and no pedestrian shall enter the roadway. Pedestrians already in the roadway shall continue to cross to the opposite sidewalk. Vehicular traffic shall yield the right of way to such pedestrians.*
    According to this regulation,

    A. if a pedestrian has just started to cross a street and the DON'T WALK signal begins to flash, the pedestrian is permitted to continue crossing
    B. pedestrians may start across a street when the DON'T WALK signal is flashing, but they should proceed rapidly
    C. pedestrians always have the right of way at an intersection
    D. if a pedestrian is in the middle of the street when the DON'T WALK signal begins to flash, he should turn around and go back

38. A regulation concerning taxicabs says that a driver of a taxicab is permitted to stand in front of a fire hydrant *where standing or parking regulations are not in effect, provided that the driver remains in the driver's seat ready for immediate operation of the taxicab at all times and starts the motor on hearing the approach of fire apparatus, and provided further that the driver shall immediately remove the taxicab from in front of the fire hydrant when instructed to do so by any member of the police, fire, or other municipal department acting in his official capacity.*
    An agent could MOST reasonably assume that this regulation

    A. prohibits agents from directing taxis except in emergency situations
    B. requires a taxidriver to keep his engine running at all times while he is standing in front of a fire hydrant
    C. shows that if a taxi is blocking a fire hydrant, firemen can probably find another hydrant nearby that they can use instead
    D. gives an agent the authority to instruct a taxi-driver to move away from a fire hydrant if the agent feels that circumstances require this action

39. Close examination of traffic accident statistics reveals that traffic accidents are frequently the result of violations of traffic laws -- and usually the violations are the result of illegal and dangerous driving behavior, rather than the result of mechanical defects or poor road conditions.
    According to this statement, the MAJORITY of dangerous traffic violations are caused by

A. poor driving
B. bad roads
C. unsafe cars
D. unwise traffic laws

40. In directing traffic, visibility is essential not only for efficient traffic control but also for the personal safety of the agent. Whistles, white gloves, and reflective vests are examples of equipment that can make an agent easily visible to both motorists and pedestrians. It is important to use this equipment and not take off a reflective vest in hot weather, for instance, or cover it up with a coat in cold weather.
    According to this statement, the BASIC reason why an agent should wear a reflective vest is that

    A. the vest is lightweight and will not be uncomfortably hot
    B. departmental regulations require wearing a vest
    C. the vest makes it easy for pedestrians and motorists to see the agent
    D. a coat can be worn over it in cold weather

40.____

MEMORY PAGES

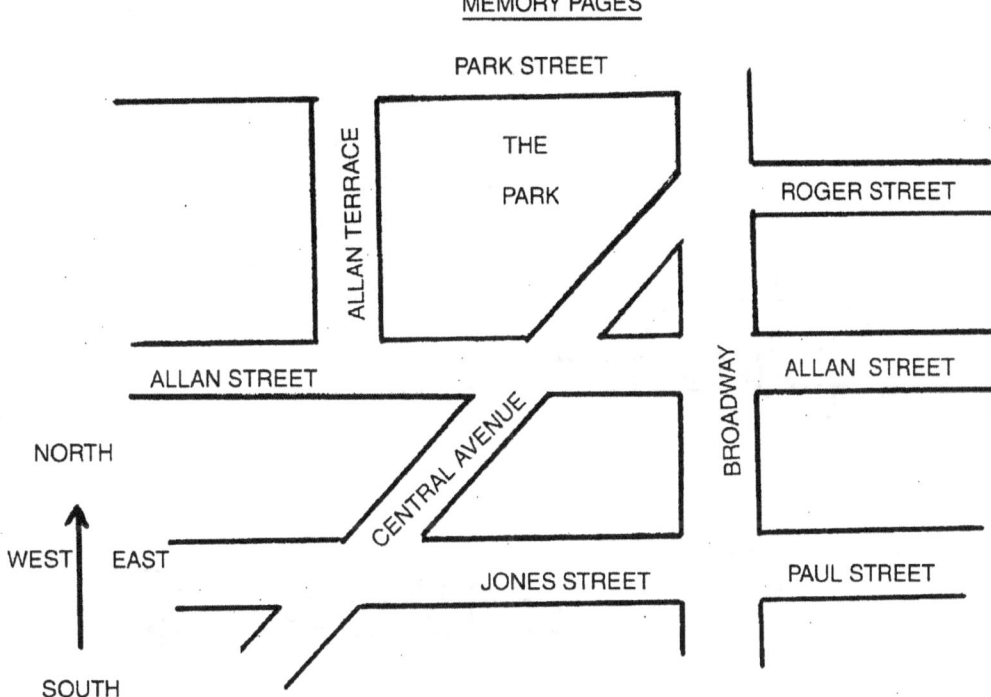

10 (#1)

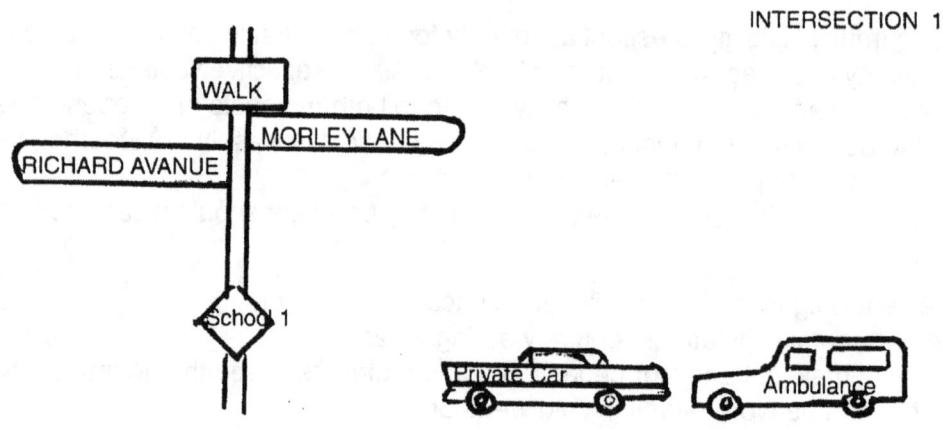

INTERSECTION 1

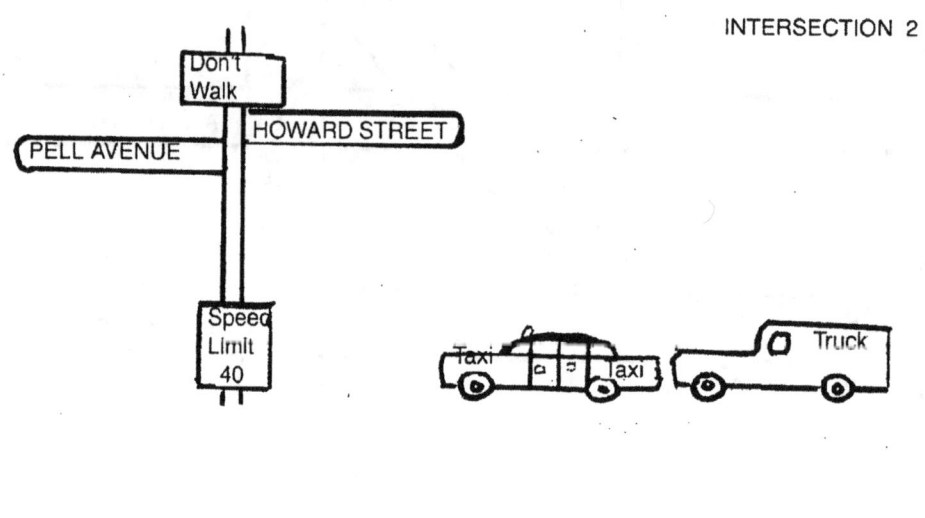

INTERSECTION 2

KEY (CORRECT ANSWERS)

1. C	11. B	21. A	31. B
2. C	12. D	22. D	32. B
3. D	13. A	23. C	33. D
4. A	14. A	24. B	34. C
5. A	15. C	25. D	35. C
6. A	16. B	26. D	36. C
7. A	17. D	27. C	37. A
8. D	18. A	28. C	38. D
9. C	19. B	29. D	39. A
10. C	20. B	30. D	40. C

TEST 2

DIRECTIONS: Each question or incomplete statement is followed by several suggested answers or completions. Select the one that BEST answers the question or completes the statement. *PRINT THE LETTER OF THE CORRECT ANSWER IN THE SPACE AT THE RIGHT.*

1. According to the law, all persons using a roadway have *equal rights.* They must all obey the rules of the road and must yield the right of way to others under many circumstances. But no one *class* of persons using the roadway has superior rights. A basic rule of equality and fair sharing applies to motor vehicle operators, pedestrians, bicycle and motorcycle riders, horseback riders, and even to people driving cattle or walking dogs along the roadway.
Which one of the following conclusions can MOST reasonably be drawn from this statement?

    A. The law says that no one should ever yield the right of way to anybody else, since everybody has equal rights.
    B. The law says that everybody using a roadway must follow the same general set of rules.
    C. Drivers of motor vehicles should have the right of way in cities under most circumstances.
    D. A small group such as motorcyclists should not have the same rights as a large group such as pedestrians.

1.___

2. In 2000, almost 55,000 people were killed in motor vehicle accidents. About 23,000 of these fatalities were the result of collisions between motor vehicles; about 14,000 were the result of vehicles overturning or running off the roadway; about 7,000 were the result of collisions with other objects; and nearly 11,000 were pedestrian deaths. Nearly two-thirds of all pedestrian deaths occurred in urban areas, and only about one-third in rural areas or suburbs.
Which one of the following conclusions is DIRECTLY supported by the information given in this statement?

    A. Almost all deaths from traffic accidents in 2000 occurred in cities.
    B. Most of the 2000 accidents in which pedestrians were killed took place in cities.
    C. Collisions between two motor vehicles do not happen very often in cities.
    D. Vehicles in cities do not run off the roadway very often.

2.___

3. Traffic laws do not say that the *intent* of the violator has any bearing on the offense. A traffic law usually makes a certain act unlawful, whether or not the person who committed the act intended to do something wrong. An explanation such as *I didn't know I was going over the speed limit* or *I didn't see the warning signal* is, therefore, no excuse at all in the eyes of the law. Following are four different explanations that a driver might give after being accused of going through a red light. Assume that the driver is telling the truth in each case.
Which of the reasons is MOST clearly *no excuse at all* in the eyes of the law?

    A. The traffic patrolman signaled me to go through.
    B. My brakes suddenly failed, without any warning.
    C. I was thinking about something else, and I didn't notice the light had changed.
    D. I swear the traffic light wasn't red it was green!

3.___

48

Questions 4-6.

DIRECTIONS: Questions 4 through 6 are to be answered on the basis of the information given in the passage below.

There is one bad habit of drivers that often causes chain collisions at traffic lights. It is the habit of keeping one foot poised over the accelerator pedal, ready to step on the gas the instant the light turns green. A driver who is watching the light -- instead of watching the cars in front of him -- may "jump the gun" and bump the car in front of him, and this car in turn may bump the next car. If a driver is resting his foot on the accelerator, his foot will be slammed down when he bumps into the car ahead. This makes the collision worse, and makes it very likely that cars further ahead in the line are going to get involved in a series of violent bumps.

4. Which of the following conclusions can MOST reasonably be drawn from the information given in the passage? 4.____

   A. American drivers have a great many bad driving habits.
   B. Drivers should step on the gas as soon as the light turns green.
   C. A driver with poor driving habits should be arrested and fined.
   D. A driver should not rest his foot on the accelerator when the car is stopped for a traffic light.

5. From the information given in the passage, a reader should be able to tell that a *chain* collision may be defined as a collision 5.____

   A. caused by bad driving habits at traffic lights
   B. in which one car hits another car, this second car hits a third car, and so on
   C. caused by drivers who fail to use their accelerators
   D. that takes place at an intersection where there is a traffic light

6. The passage states that a driver who watches the light instead of paying attention to traffic may 6.____

   A. be involved in an accident
   B. end up in jail
   C. lose his license
   D. develop bad driving habits

Questions 7-14.

DIRECTIONS: Questions 7 through 14 are to be answered on the basis of the code table and the instructions given below.

Code Letter for Traffic Problem	B	H	Q	J	F	L	M	I
Code Number for Action Taken	1	2	3	4	5	6	7	8

Assume that each of the capital letters on the above chart is a radio code for a particular traffic problem and that the number immediately below each capital letter is the radio code for the correct action to be taken to deal with the problem. For instance, *1* is the action to be taken to deal with problem *B; 2* is the action to be taken to deal with problem *H*, and so forth.

In each question, a series of code letters is given in Column I. Column 2 gives four different arrangements of code numbers. You are to pick the answer (A, B, C, or D) in Column 2 that gives the code numbers that match the code letters in the same order.

SAMPLE QUESTION:

Column 1
BHLFMQ

Column 2
A. 125678
B. 216573
C. 127653
D. 126573

According to the chart, the code numbers that correspond to these code letters are as follows: B-I, H-2, L-6, F-5, M - 7, Q - 3. Therefore, the right answer is 126573. This answer is D in Column 2.

Column 1

7. BHQLMI
8. HBJQLF
9. QHMLFJ
10. FLQJIM
11. FBIHMJ
12. MIHFQB
13. JLFHQIM

Column 2

7.
A. 123456
B. 123567
C. 123678
D. 125678

8.
A. 214365
B. 213456
C. 213465
D. 214387

9.
A. 321654
B. 345678
C. 327645
D. 327654

10.
A. 543287
B. 563487
C. 564378
D. 654378

11.
A. 518274
B. 152874
C. 528164
D. 517842

12.
A. 872341
B. 782531
C. 782341
D. 783214

13.
A. 465237
B. 456387
C. 4652387
D. 4562387

Column 1   Column 2

14. LBJQIFH
      A. 6143852
      B. 6134852
      C. 61437852
      D. 61431852

14.____

15. Add the following numbers: 17 1/2, 29 1/2, and 6 1/2.
 The correct total is

 A. 32   B. 42   C. 53 1/2   D. 96 1/2

15.____

16. Add 1,516 and 3,497; then subtract 766.
 The correct answer is

 A. 2,731   B. 4,247   C. 5,357   D. 5,779

16.____

17. Add 39, 24, and 36. Then divide the total by 3.
 The correct answer is

 A. 23   B. 33   C. 96   D. 99

17.____

18. An agent has written out 29 summonses for moving violations, 13 summonses for parking violations, and 3 sumnonses for other violations.
 The total number of summonses he has written out is

 A. 36   B. 42   C. 43   D. 45

18.____

19. A driver complains about being ticketed for parking too near a fire hydrant. He insists that his car is *at least 8 yards from the hydrant.*
 If he is right, how far away from the hydrant is the car, in terms of *feet* rather than yards?
 _____ feet.

 A. 16   B. 24   C. 30   D. 80

19.____

20. At the intersection of an avenue and a cross street, the traffic lights have been set so that traffic on the avenue has a green light for 55 seconds followed by a yellow light for 5 seconds, then traffic on the cross street has a green light for 25 seconds followed by a yellow light for 5 seconds.
 How long is a complete cycle of lights at this intersection -- that is, how much time must pass from the moment the light turns from red to green, until the moment the light will turn from red to green again?
 _____ seconds.

 A. 60   B. 70   C. 80   D. 90

20.____

21. An agent has jotted down the following notes on one day's work:
      8:00-11:30 On duty at intersection as assigned
      11:30-12:00 Off duty - lunch
      12:00- 2:00 On duty - attending assigned training session

      2:00- 4:00 On duty at intersection - replacement came late
 How many ON-DUTY hours do this agent's notes show for this particular day?
 _____ hours.

 A. 4   B. 7   C. 7 1/2   D. 8

21.____

22. If a traffic jam of 78 vehicles occurs at the intersection you are controlling, and if one car can pass through the intersection every 10 seconds, how LONG will it take to clear these 78 vehicles out of the intersection?
    _____ minutes.

    A. 5.2   B. 7.8   C. 13.0   D. 15.7

23. An agent issued the following summonses in one day: 12 summonses at $25 each, 5 summonses at $15 each, and 3 summonses at $10 each.
    What is the TOTAL amount of the fines for the summonses he gave out on that day?

    A. $305   B. $315   C. $405   D. $485

Questions 24-27.

DIRECTIONS: Questions 24 through 27 are to be answered on the basis of the chart below which provides information about the current assignments of a group of agents.

Name of Agent	Code No. of Assignment	Date Assigned	Section No.	Name of Supervisor
Estes, Jerome	34-08-A	10/8/09	F0281	H. Landon
Gomez, Margie	34-07-A	10/15/09	F0281	S. Lee
Isaac, John	32-07-B	10/8/09	F0381	R. Puente
Kaplan, Pearl	32-07-A	11/5/09	F0381	R. Puente
Kapler, Peter	34-05-A	10/22/09	F0281	S. Lee
Karell, Peter	42-05-A	11/12/09	F1281	T. Pujol

24. Two of the agents received their current assignments on the same date.
    This date is _____, 2009.

    A. October 8
    B. October 15
    C. October 22
    D. November 12

25. Which of the following is Peter Kapler's section number?

    A. 34-05-A   B. 42-05-A   C. F0281   D. F1281

26. R. Puente is the supervisor for

    A. only John Isaac
    B. only John Isaac and Pearl Kaplan
    C. John Isaac, Pearl Kaplan, and Peter Kapler
    D. John Isaac, Pearl Kaplan, and Peter Karell

27. How many of the agents were given their current assignments BEFORE November 1, 2009?

    A. 2   B. 4   C. 5   D. 6

6 (#2)

Questions 28-31.

DIRECTIONS: Questions 28 through 31 are based on the Fact Situation and the Traffic Control Report form below. Read the Fact Situation careful, and examine the blank report form. Questions 28 through 31 ask how the report form should be filled in, based on the information given in the Fact Situation.

FACT SITUATION

Mary Fields is a Traffic Control Agent. Her city employee number is Z90019. She is assigned to duty at the intersection of Silver Street and Amber Avenue. On the morning of May 15, she arrives at this intersection at 8:00 A.M. and sees that there is a new "patch job" on the surface of Amber Avenue in the middle of the pedestrian crosswalk and near the northwest corner of the intersection. The day before, an emergency crew was digging here. The hole is now closed and re-surfaced, but the patch job on the surface was not done very well. The patch is nearly an inch higher than the surrounding surface, and it has a sharp edge that pedestrians are likely to trip on. Mary Fields thinks this condition is dangerous, and she reports it on the Traffic Control Report form.

```
TRAFFIC CONTROL REPORT:
DEFECTIVE EQUIPMENT OR UNSAFE CONDITION

1. Date of observation _____  2. Time _____
3. Exact Location _____
4. Type of equipment or condition found or unsafe to be defective
   or unsafe _____
5. Type of defect _____
6. Name of reporting Agent _____
7. Employee No. _____  8. Precinct No _____
```

28. Which of the following should be entered in Blank 3?

    A. Silver Street at Amber Avenue, near northeast corner
    B. Silver Street at Amber Avenue, near northwest corner
    C. Amber Avenue at Silver Street, near northeast corner
    D. Amber Avenue at Silver Street, near northwest corner

29. Which of the following should be entered in Blank 4?

    A. Pedestrian traffic signals
    B. Pedestrian crosswalk markings
    C. Surface patch
    D. Unsafe condition

30. The information call for in Blank 5 is needed to determine what kind of repairs must be made and what kind of repair crew must be sent.
    Which of the following entries for Blank 5 will be MOST useful to the people who receive this report in deciding what kind of repair crew to assign to the job?

A. Pedestrians may stumble and fall.
B. New patch is higher than rest of surface
C. Emergency crew dug a hole here.
D. Street repairs were not done very well.

31. There is one blank on the form for which the Fact Situation does not provide the information needed.
    The blank that CANNOT be filled out on the basis of the information given is Blank

    A. 2   B. 6   C. 7   D. 8

Questions 32-35.

DIRECTIONS: Questions 32 through 35 are based on the Fact Sheet that appears below. Examine the Fact Sheet carefully. Then answer Questions 32 through 35 on the basis of the information given on the sheet.

```
FACT SHEET #T - 3010

Date  5/19           Time  8:39 A.M.      Code   L-90
Place  3.9 W. 38 Street                   County  N.Y.
Type of violation    Parked in front of Hydrant

Vehicle:                              Operator or owner
  Make  Dodge   Color  Green   Type  Truck   Name _____
  plate  123 ZYX                            License no. _____

Fine for ttt violation : $10__ $20__ $25 x  Other $_____
Report  submitted  by   Manuel Sanchez
```

32. The violation reported on the Fact Sheet is a violation of a

    A. speed limit regulation
    B. regulation concerning traffic signals
    C. regulation concerning driver licenses
    D. parking regulation

33. The vehicle involved in the violation was a

    A. Dodge car   B. black car
    C. blue truck   D. Dodge truck

34. The section of the Fact Sheet which is NOT filled in asks for information about the

    A. operator or owner of the vehicle
    B. amount of the fine
    C. place where the violation occurred
    D. person submitting the report

35. Like most standard reporting forms, Fact Sheet #T-3010 can be used only to report certain kinds of situations. It would be LEAST appropriate to use Fact Sheet #T-3010 to report which one of the following incidents?
    A

A. driver goes through a red light
B. delivery truck blocks a traffic lane while unloading merchandise
C. pedestrian has a heart attack
D. bus driver stops to let a passenger off in the middle of a block where there is no bus stop marked

Questions 36-39.

DIRECTIONS: Questions 36 through 39 are to be answered on the basis of the following map.

The circle with an arrow (↑) represents you. Assume that you are walking - not driving - and that the arrow on the circle shows the direction in which you are presently facing.

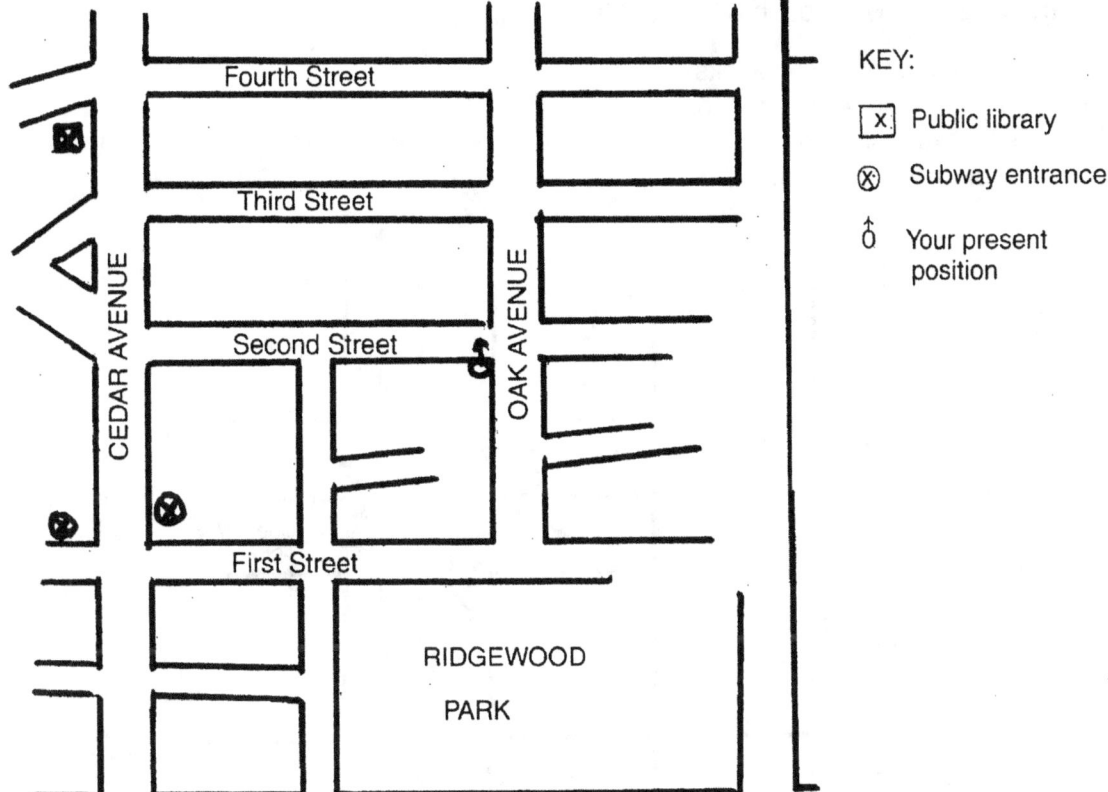

36. How would you get to Ridgewood Park from the place where you are now standing, according to the map?

    A. Walk one block in the direction opposite to that which you are facing
    B. Turn to your left, then walk one block
    C. Turn to your right, then walk one block
    D. Just walk straight ahead for one block

37. Which of the following sets of directions would take you CLOSEST to the nearest subway entrance from your original position on the map?

    A. Turn to your left, then walk two blocks straight ahead
    B. Turn to your right and walk two blocks, then turn left and walk another block

C. Turn to your left and walk two blocks, then turn left again and walk one block
D. Go two blocks straight ahead, then turn right and walk another block

38. From your original position on the map, which of the following sets of directions would take you CLOSEST to the public library?

    A. Walk two blocks straight ahead, then right for two blocks
    B. Go to your left for one block, then left for another block
    C. Go two blocks straight ahead, then right for one block
    D. Go two blocks straight ahead, then turn left and walk one block

39. Although 8th Street is not shown on this map, common sense can tell you how to get there from your original position on the map.
    You are MOST likely to reach 8th Street if you walk

    A. straight ahead for six blocks
    B. straight ahead for seven blocks
    C. five blocks to your right
    D. four blocks to your left

40.

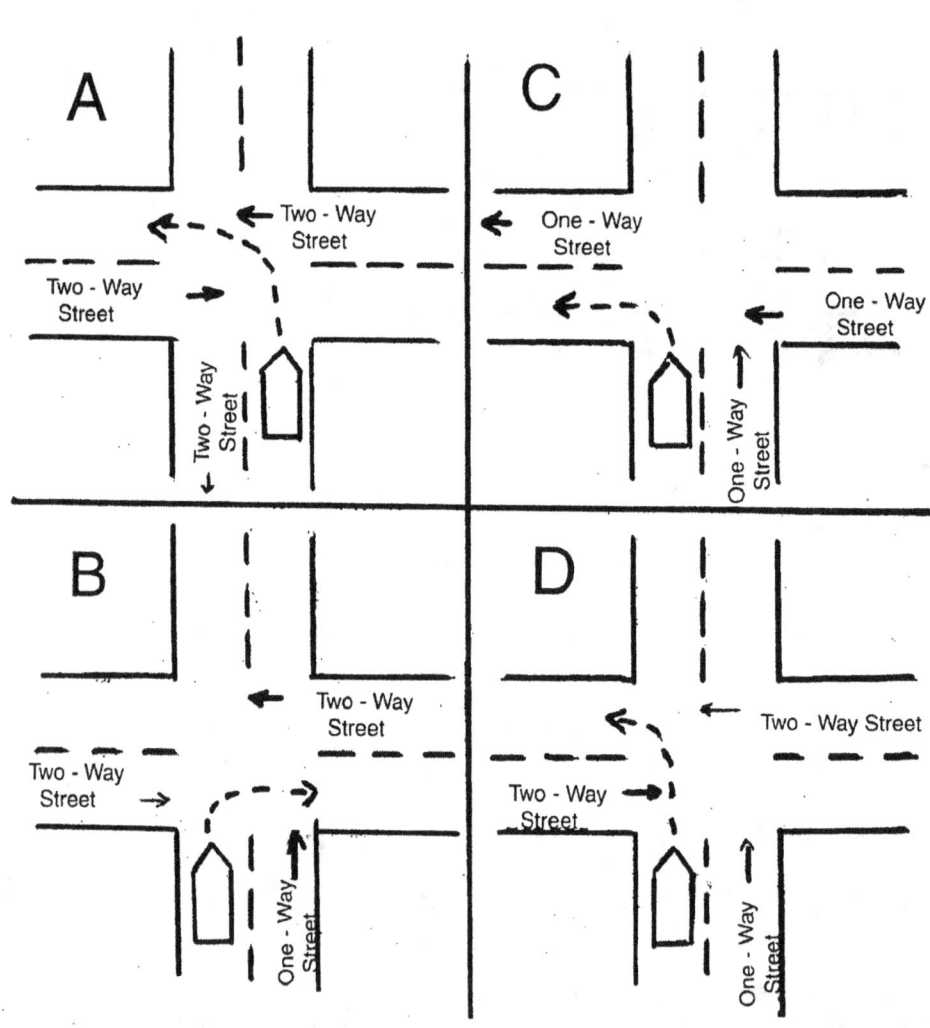

10 (#2)

The above diagrams show four different ways of making a turn into a cross street. In each diagram, the solid line represents the curb and the straight broken line is the center line of the road. Arrows are placed to show the movement of the vehicle and the direction of traffic in the various lanes. All the diagrams except one show correct ways to make a turn.
Which diagram shows an INCORRECT way to make a turn?

A. A   B. B   C. C   D. D

KEY (CORRECT ANSWERS)

1. B	11. A	21. C	31. D
2. B	12. B	22. C	32. D
3. C	13. C	23. C	33. D
4. D	14. A	24. A	34. A
5. B	15. C	25. C	35. C
6. A	16. B	26. B	36. A
7. C	17. B	27. B	37. C
8. A	18. D	28. D	38. D
9. D	19. B	29. C	39. A
10. B	20. D	30. B	40. B

EXAMINATION SECTION
TEST 1

DIRECTIONS: Each question or incomplete statement is followed by several suggested answers or completions. Select the one that BEST answers the question or completes the statement. *PRINT THE LETTER OF THE CORRECT ANSWER IN THE SPACE AT THE RIGHT.*

1. Your car's brakes transform one type of energy into another. Which of the following BEST describes the change?

   A. Kinetic energy into heat
   B. Centrifugal force into force of impact
   C. Gravity into kinetic energy
   D. Centrifugal force into heat

   1._____

2. Which of the following qualities is MOST important in driving a motor vehicle?

   A. Fast reaction time B. Courage
   C. Skill   D. Judgment

   2._____

3. Glaring headlights add to night driving hazards. Which of the following should you NOT do?

   A. Lower your headlight beams in advance of meeting other cars
   B. Reduce your speed when facing headlight glare
   C. Focus your eyes downward on the center line of the road instead of up into the oncoming lights
   D. Lower your headlight beams when following another car

   3._____

4. The following institutions lend money for the purchase of cars. Which charges the LOWEST rate of interest?

   A. Banks
   B. Pawnshops
   C. Installment finance companies
   D. Personal loan companies

   4._____

5. Under what conditions do we find the GREATEST traction?

   A. Wet concrete pavement
   B. Dry concrete pavement
   C. Dry concrete pavement with sand on it
   D. Bumpy, uneven pavement

   5._____

6. Your danger zone is

   A. the longest distance at which you can see and recognize danger
   B. your stopping distance
   C. the distance at which a vehicle in back of your car is following
   D. your braking distance

   6._____

7. For sound financing of a purchase of an automobile, you would have to raise a down payment of AT LEAST _____ of the value of the car.

    A. 10 percent   B. 25 percent
    C. one-third   D. one-half

7.____

8. Which of the following is characteristic of older paved roads and not of modern highways?

    A. Median strips   B. High road crowns
    C. Road banking   D. Long sight distances

8.____

9. Designed especially for slowing down to prepare to leave the freeway is the

    A. deceleration lane   B. median strip
    C. ramp   D. road shoulder

9.____

10. When you find yourself getting very sleepy while driving on a long trip, the BEST remedy is

    A. black coffee   B. fresh air
    C. Benzedrine   D. sleep

10.____

11. Which of these four types of insurance does a bank or other lender require the purchaser to have?

    A. Collision   B. Comprehensive
    C. Liability   D. Medical payment

11.____

12. The professional specialist who plans the operation of highways is the

    A. Commissioner of Motor Vehicles
    B. highway engineer
    C. traffic engineer
    D. Commissioner of State Police

12.____

13. Which of the following is the CORRECT formula?

    A. Braking distance + stopping distance = reaction distance
    B. Reaction distance + stopping distance = braking distance
    C. Reaction distance + braking distance = stopping distance
    D. Reaction distance + danger zone = stopping distance

13.____

14. Which of the following is a YIELD sign?

    A. (diamond-shaped sign)   B. (rectangular sign)   C. (octagonal sign)   D. (triangular sign)

14.____

15. When you drive around a curve, which of the following helps you to do it safely?

    A. Centrifugal force   B. Friction
    C. Kinetic energy   D. Force of impact

15.____

16. If you are involved in an accident, which of the following things should you NOT do? 16._____

    A. Show your driver's license and vehicle registration card and make note of the information on those of the driver of the other car.
    B. If any person seems to be seriously injured, place him in your car immediately and proceed at once to the nearest hospital.
    C. Submit accident reports as indicated by your state and local regulations.
    D. Notify your insurance company.

17. No person should drive in dense fog unless it is absolutely necessary. When it does prove necessary, he should use 17._____

    A. parking lights
    B. high-beam headlights
    C. low-beam headlights
    D. no lights, to avoid distortion of vision

18. Under which of the following would you classify the wearing of glasses to aid vision? 18._____

    A. Compensation   B. Field of vision
    C. Correction   D. Adjustment

19. The key words for driving on a slippery surface are 19._____

    A. firmly and accurately   B. gently and gradually
    C. strongly and steadily   D. quickly and surely

20. Which of the following types of insurance is MOST important to a car owner? 20._____

    A. Collision   B. Liability
    C. Comprehensive   D. Medical payment

KEY (CORRECT ANSWERS)

1.	C	11.	A
2.	D	12.	C
3.	D	13.	C
4.	A	14.	D
5.	B	15.	A
6.	B	16.	B
7.	C	17.	C
8.	B	18.	C
9.	A	19.	B
10.	D	20.	B

TEST 2

DIRECTIONS: Each question or incomplete statement is followed by several suggested answers or completions. Select the one that BEST answers the question or completes the statement. *PRINT THE LETTER OF THE CORRECT ANSWER IN THE SPACE AT THE RIGHT.*

1. Which of these four items is a *grade separation*?

    A. A divided highway
    B. A change in the slope of a hill
    C. Bushes planted between two roadways on which traffic moves in opposite directions
    D. A cloverleaf

    1.___

2. Which of the following blood alcohol concentrations should be used to establish that a driver is *under the influence of alcohol*?

    A. 0.05%   B. 0.10%   C. 0.15%   D. 0.6%

    2.___

3. Three of the following four statements are true of freeways. Which statement is NOT true?

    A. They have a limited number of interchanges at which vehicles may enter or leave the freeway.
    B. They have a limited number of STOP and GO signals.
    C. Traffic moving in opposite directions is not separated by a median strip.
    D. Crossing the median strip is not permitted.

    3.___

4. To correct a skid, you should

    A. steer in the direction in which the rear of the car is skidding
    B. steer in the direction opposite that in which the rear of the car is skidding
    C. hold the steering wheel firmly in the straight-ahead position
    D. use the parking or handbrake so that only the rear wheels will lock while the front wheels turn freely

    4.___

5. The MOST dangerous effects of alcohol on the driver are those concerned with

    A. vision
    B. reaction time
    C. behavior
    D. coordination and driving skill

    5.___

6. The *Three E's* of traffic safety are included in the following four words. Which of them is NOT one of the *Three E's*?

    A. Education   B. Engineering
    C. Enforcement   D. Efficiency

    6.___

7. Which of the following BEST describes the true meaning of the word *courage*?

    A. Ability to overcome fear
    B. Absence of fear
    C. Taking chances to gain a reputation as a daredevil
    D. Lack of realization of the true nature of danger

    7.___

8. Which of the following types of insurance is of GREATEST importance to you when you own a car?

   A. Liability
   B. Collision
   C. Comprehensive
   D. Medical payment

9. Which of the following statements is NOT correct?

   A. Most states have legalized the use of electric directional signals to signal turns.
   B. Overheating is always due to failures in the cooling system.
   C. Power brakes do not decrease the stopping distance.
   D. The horn should never be sounded except in the interest of safety.

10. Three of the following are good safety features. Which is NOT a safety feature?

    A. Door locks
    B. Rear-view mirror inside the car
    C. Eye-level outside mirror
    D. Ventilation of the inside of the car

11. The MOST important factor in good car maintenance is

    A. an honest, dependable service station or garage
    B. a skilled mechanic
    C. high quality, reliable parts
    D. a responsible car owner

12. Three of the following procedures will add to tire traction in starting your car on ice. Which one will NOT help?

    A. Letting some air out of the rear tires
    B. Sprinkling sand on the ice
    C. Slipping the clutch
    D. Feeding gas more gently and more gradually

13. The four-stroke cycle includes THREE of the following. Which of the following is NOT part of the cycle? _____ stroke.

    A. Intake
    B. Compression
    C. Power
    D. Completion

14. Vehicles A, C, and D in the illustration shown at the right have stopped to allow vehicle B to turn.
    Which vehicle, A, C, or D, would be the FIRST to cross the intersection, considering right-of-way rules?

    A. A
    B. C
    C. D
    D. None of the above

15. What part of the cost of planning, designing, and constructing the National System of Interstate and Defense Highways is paid for by Federal-aid funds?   15.____

   A. 90%   B. 50%   C. 10%   D. 100%

16. When you leave a freeway and drive on a city street, you must check your speed frequently because you may be   16.____

   A. accelerated
   B. suffering from highway hypnosis
   C. velocitized
   D. suffering impairment of vision due to carbon monoxide

17. Which of the following statements is CORRECT?   17.____

   A. Certain drugs, like Benzedrine in *keep-awake* pills, actually make driving at night safe.
   B. A driver should trust no one but a physician to determine whether or not he should drive after taking any kind of drug.
   C. The Federal Food and Drug Act does not permit the sale of any drug dangerous to a driver without a prescription from a registered physician.
   D. The individual driver must rely entirely upon his judgment and knowledge of how a specific drug will affect him.

18. Three of the following four maintenance procedures are good. Which is NOT a good procedure?   18.____

   A. Rotate your tires to avoid uneven wear.
   B. Avoid letting oil or gasoline come into contact with your tires.
   C. For driving in very hot weather, underinflate your tires to avoid building up excessive pressure in them.
   D. Keep the battery terminals covered with a light layer of grease.

19. Drivers should be able to recognize traffic signs by their shape. Which of the following signs warns drivers that they are approaching a railroad grade crossing?   19.____

   A.   B.   C.   D.

20. Imagine that the steering wheel is the face of a clock. The driver's hands should grasp it at _____ and _____ o'clock.   20.____

   A. 8; 4   B. 9; 3   C. 10; 2   D. 11; 1

KEY (CORRECT ANSWERS)

1. D
2. A
3. B
4. A
5. D

6. C
7. A
8. A
9. B
10. C

11. C
12. A
13. D
14. C
15. A

16. C
17. B
18. C
19. B
20. C

TRAFFIC CONTROL STUDIES

CONTENTS

	Page
Traffic Control Device Studies	1
Vehicle Registration Study	1
Origin-Destination Study	1
Speed Study	1
Speed-Delay Study	1
Motor Vehicle Volume Study	2
Roadway Capacity Studies	2
Vehicle Occupancy Study	2
Pedestrian Study	2
Observance of Stop Sign Study	3
Observance of Traffic Signals Study	3
Parking Studies	3
Accident Records Study	3

TRAFFIC CONTROL STUDIES

Type	Purpose	Requirement For Study	Personnel and Equipment
Traffic Control Device Studies	To inventory, locate, classify, and evaluate traffic control devices; and increase adequacy of these devices.	One initial study of all devices which is updated by periodic studies of specific areas on a routine basis.	Special two-man teams. Normal patrol equipment, and stopwatch, tape measure (100 ft), manual on uniform traffic control devices, field forms or notebook.
Vehicle Registration Study	To determine peak loads of traffic and adequacy of parking. May be used to adjust or update origin and destination study, or be used in lieu of this study.	As required to measure peak traffic in relation to existing roadways, and duty hour schedules.	Study is conducted by extraction and processing of information with ADPS. Traffic section personnel obtain input data, and ADP section processes data as required.
Origin-Destination Study	To develop data on origins and destinations of personnel entering, leaving, or traveling within an installation on a typical working day.	As required to support long-range planning, to anticipate major changes in strengths and functions, to support traffic construction requirements, and to assign traffic properly.	Varies with type and scope of study.
Speed Study	To determine if prevailing speeds are proper, to determine proper speed for new or improve roadways; to serve as a warrant for, and guide in, the placement and operation of traffic control devices, and to assist in accident research and enforcement.	Conducted for specific roadways as a result of observation, enforcement activity, and accident experience. Also required for new or renovated roadways.	Personnel may consist of one-man or two-man teams depending on the method and type of study. Equipment may consist of patrol vehicle, mirror box, stopwatch, field sheets, radar (with or without graphic recorder), and electric timer. Normally, police gear and marked vehicles are not used.
Speed-Delay Study	To determine variation in speed along a route; indicate amount, location, course, frequency and duration of delays, and provide overall speed and travel time along a route.	Conducted on specific routes as problems develop of congestion, delay and insufficient capacity. Also conducted when necessary to assign route priority, to consider use of alternate routes, to evaluate speed limits, and to check effectiveness of control devices.	Personnel will consist of a two-man team without distinctive police gear. Unmarked sedan or ¼-ton truck, standard watch and stopwatch, and field sheets as required.

Type	Purpose	Requirement For Study	Personnel and Equipment
Motor Vehicle Volume Study	To obtain an accurate record of the number, directional movements, and variation in volume of motor vehicles passing through intersections or using major routes, and to provide data for use in construction of a traffic flow map.	Conducted as required to determine street adequacy, to appraise effectiveness of traffic control measures, and to establish priorities and designs for traffic and/or road improvements and for new streets.	Two policemen are required to observe and record at a normal two-way intersection. If traffic exceeds 1500 vehicles per hour entering the intersection, one policeman may be required for each of the four approaches. Ordinary watches, field sheets, summary sheets, and (if used) manual counters are needed.
Roadway Capacity Studies	To determine the practical capacities of roadways as an adjunct to other studies; and to provide basic information required to update traffic regulations, to establish priorities for street improvements, and to aid in traffic planning.	Conducted as required to relieve congestion through appropriate corrective action in those areas where traffic volumes exceed traffic capacities.	Varies with scope of study. Normally, as a minimum, requires a two-man team equipped with tape measure, stopwatch post or engineer maps, sketch pads, and odometer (optional).
Vehicle Occupancy Study	To determine the number of occupants per motor vehicle.	As required to examine parking difficulties and congestion; to assist in planning for future traffic and parking facilities, and to evaluate the adequacy of transit services.	Either one-man or two-man teams with normal police gear depending on traffic volume. Equipment required includes ordinary watch, field sheets, and summary sheets.
Pedestrian Study	To determine the amount of pedestrian traffic at intersections and/or midblock crossing points.	As required to evaluate pedestrian-vehicle conflicts, and assist in planning control, physical protection, and enforcement measures.	Locally designed field sheets or notebooks. Either one-man or two-man teams depending on the pedestrian volume. Police gear is not worn.
Observance of Stop Sign Study	To determine the degree of drive obedience.	As required to study the relation of driver obedience to accidents at high accident frequency locations, and to assist in taking measures to increase driver obedience.	One person can normally make this study. He should not wear distinctive police equipment and should have a watch and field sheets.

Type	Purpose	Requirement For Study	Personnel and Equipment
Observance of Traffic Signals Study	To determine voluntary observance of intersection traffic control signals.	As required at intersections where congestion and high accident rates prevail.	Two policemen without distinctive police gear are normally required. On multiple approaches with heavy traffic, four or six policemen may be required. Equipment consists of an ordinary watch, field sheets, and summary sheets.
Parking Studies	To determine the adequacy, use, and location of existing parking facilities; and to provide guidance in the placement and design of parking areas for future use.	A comprehensive, installation survey is normally required only in conjunction with long-range planning for major changes in the installation. Surveys are conducted at specific areas as parking problems become evident, or in anticipation of the development of parking problems.	Field sheets, summary sheets, post map, aerial photos, and questionnaires are used as required for the specific study or survey being conducted. Personnel requirements and use of police gear depend on the type and scope of the study.
Accident Records Study	To improve enforcement, engineering, and education programs.	As needed to identify and treat high accident locations, to assist in evaluating highway design factors, to establish priorities of action, and to measure effectiveness of remedial action.	ADP equipment and trained personnel for automatic data processing. Normally, two police perform observations for condition and collision diagrams.

HIGHWAY TRAFFIC SIGNALS

CONTENTS

Page

A. General

Section A- 1. Types — 1
A- 2. Basis of Installation — 1

B. Traffic Control Signals

Section B- 1. General Aspects — 1
B- 2. Area of Control — 1
B- 3. Advantages and Disadvantages of Traffic Control Signals — 2
B- 4. Portable Traffic Control Signals — 2
B- 5. Meaning of Signal Indications — 2
B- 6. Application of Signal Indications — 4
B- 7. Number of Lenses per Signal Face — 6
B- 8. Size and Design of Signal Lenses — 6
B- 9. Arrangement of Lenses in Signal Faces — 7
B-10. Illumination of Lenses — 9
B-11. Visibility and Shielding of Signal Faces — 10
B-12. Number and Locations of Signal Faces — 10
B-13. Height of Signal Faces — 13
B-14. Transverse Location of Traffic Signal Supports and Controller Cabinets — 13
B-15. Vehicle Change Interval — 14
B-16. Unexpected Conflicts During Green Interval — 14
B-17. Coordination of Traffic Control Signals — 15
B-18. Flashing Operation of Traffic Control Signals — 15
B-19. Continuity of Operation — 16
B-20. Signal Operation Must Relate to Traffic Flow — 16
B-21. Traffic Signals Near Grade Crossings — 16
B-22. Emergency Operation of Traffic Signals — 17
B-23. Maintenance of Traffic Control Signals — 18
B-24. Painting — 19
B-25. Vehicle Detectors — 19
B-26. Auxiliary Signs — 19
B-27. Removal of Confusing Advertising Lights — 20

HIGHWAY TRAFFIC SIGNALS

A. GENERAL

A-1 Types

This part relates to a group of devices called highway traffic signals. These devices include: traffic control signals, beacons, lane-use control signals, drawbridge signals, emergency traffic control signals and train approach signals and gates. Only the first of these will be discussed in this section.

A-2 Basis of Installation

In most cases the installation of a highway traffic control signal will operate either to the advantage or disadvantage of the vehicles and persons controlled. A careful analysis of traffic operations and other factors at a large number of signalized and unsignalized intersections, coupled with the judgment of experienced engineers, have provided a series of warrants that define the minimum conditions under which signal installations may be justified. Consequently the selection and use of this control device should be preceded by a thorough engineering study of roadway and traffic conditions.

Engineering studies should be made of operating signals to determine if the type of installation and the timing program meet the current requirements of traffic.

B. TRAFFIC CONTROL SIGNALS

B-1 General Aspects

There are two types of traffic control signals, pretimed and traffic-actuated.

The features of traffic control signals in which vehicle operators and pedestrians are interested are the location, design, indications, and legal significance of the signals. These are identical for all types of traffic control signals. Uniformity in the design features that affect the traffic to be controlled (as set forth in this Manual) is especially important for safe and efficient traffic operations.

Special police supervision and/or enforcement should be provided for a new non-intersection location.

B-2 Area of Control

A traffic control signal shall control traffic only at the intersection or mid-block location where the installation is placed.

B-3 Advantages and Disadvantages of Traffic Control Signals

Traffic control signals are valuable devices for the control of vehicle and pedestrian traffic. However, because they assign the right-of-way to the various traffic movements, traffic control signals exert a profound influence on traffic flow.

Traffic control signals, properly located and operated usually have one or more of the following advantages:

1. They can provide for the orderly movement of traffic.
2. Where proper physical layouts and control measures are used, they can increase the traffic-handling capacity of the intersection.
3. They can reduce the frequency of certain types of accidents, especially the right-angle type.
4. Under favorable conditions, they can be coordinated to provide for continuous or nearly continuous movement of traffic at a definite speed along a given route.
5. They can be used to interrupt heavy traffic at intervals to permit other traffic, vehicular or pedestrian, to cross.

Many laymen believe that traffic signals provide the solution to all traffic problems at intersections. This has led to their installation at a large number of locations where no legitimate factual warrant exists.

Traffic signal installations, even though warranted by traffic and roadway conditions, can be ill-designed, ineffectively placed, improperly operated, or poorly maintained. The following factors can result from improper or unwarranted signal installations:

1. Excessive delay may be caused.
2. Disobedience of the signal indications is encouraged.
3. The use of less adequate routes may be induced in an attempt to avoid such signals.
4. Accident frequency (especially the rear-end type) can be significantly increased.

B-4 Portable Traffic Control Signals

A portable traffic control signal not meeting all the requirements is not recognized as a standard traffic control device.

B-5 Meaning of Signal Indications

The following meanings shall be given to highway traffic signal indications, except those on pedestrian signals:

1. Green indications shall have the following meanings:

   a. Traffic, except pedestrians, facing a CIRCULAR GREEN may proceed straight through or turn right or left unless a sign at such place prohibits either such turn. But vehicular traffic, including vehicles turning right or left, shall yield the right-of-way to other vehicles, and to pedestrians lawfully within the intersection or an adjacent crosswalk, at the time such signal is exhibited.

b. Traffic, except pedestrians, facing a GREEN ARROW, shown alone or in combination with another indication, may cautiously enter the intersection only to make the movement indicated by such arrow, or such other movement as is permitted by other indications shown at the same time. Such vehicular traffic shall yield the right-of-way to pedestrians lawfully within an adjacent crosswalk and to other traffic lawfully using the intersection.

c. Unless otherwise directed by a pedestrian signal, pedestrians facing any green indication, except when the sole green indication is a turn arrow, may proceed across the roadway within any marked or unmarked crosswalk.

2. Steady yellow indications shall have the following meanings:

a. Traffic, except pedestrians, facing a steady CIRCULAR YELLOW or YELLOW ARROW signal is thereby warned that the related green movement is being terminated or that a red indication will be exhibited immediately thereafter when vehicular traffic shall not enter the intersection.

b. Pedestrians facing a steady CIRCULAR YELLOW or YELLOW ARROW signal, unless otherwise directed by a pedestrian signal, are thereby advised that there is insufficient time to cross the roadway before a red indication is shown and no pedestrian shall then start to cross the roadway.

3. Steady red indications shall have the following meanings:

a. Traffic, except pedestrians, facing a steady CIRCULAR RED signal alone shall stop at a clearly marked stop line, but if none, before entering the crosswalk on the near side of the intersection, or if none, then before entering the intersection and shall remain standing until an indication to proceed is shown except as provided in b below.

b. When a sign is in place permitting a turn, traffic, except pedestrians, facing a steady CIRCULAR RED signal may cautiously enter the intersection to make the turn indicated by such sign after stopping as provided in a above. Such vehicular traffic shall yield the right-of-way to pedestrians lawfully within an adjacent crosswalk and to other traffic lawfully using the intersection.

c. Unless otherwise directed by a pedestrian signal, pedestrians facing a steady CIRCULAR RED signal alone shall not enter the roadway.

d. Traffic, except pedestrians, facing a steady RED ARROW indication may not enter the intersection to make the movement indicated by such arrow, and unless entering the intersection to make such other movement as is permitted by other indications shown at the same time, shall stop at a clearly marked stop line, but if none, before entering the crosswalk on the near side of the intersection, or if none, then before entering the intersection and shall remain standing until an indication to make the movement indicated by such arrow is shown.

e. Unless otherwise directed by a pedestrian signal, pedestrians facing a steady RED ARROW signal indication shall not enter the roadway.

4. Flashing signal indications shall have the following meanings:

a. Flashing red (stop signal)—When a red lens is illuminated with rapid intermittent flashes, drivers of vehicles shall stop at a clearly marked stop line, but if none, before entering the crosswalk on the near side of the intersection, or if none, then at the point nearest the intersecting roadway where the driver has a view of approaching traffic on the intersecting roadway before entering the intersection, and the right to proceed shall be subject to the rules applicable after making a stop at a STOP sign.

b. Flashing yellow (caution signal)—When a yellow lens is illuminated with rapid intermittent flashes, drivers of vehicles may proceed through the intersection or past such signal only with caution.

B-6 Application of Signal Indications

Basic displays used in signal operations are the steady CIRCULAR RED, CIRCULAR YELLOW or CIRCULAR GREEN indication, used on each of the approaches. The application for these signal indications shall be as follows:

1. A steady CIRCULAR RED indication:

a. Shall be given when it is intended to prohibit traffic from entering the intersection or other controlled area.

b. Should be displayed with the appropriate green arrow indications when it is intended to permit traffic to make a specified turn or turns, and to prohibit traffic from proceeding straight ahead through the controlled area. This display is optional where it is physically impossible for traffic to go straight ahead, as at the head of a "T" intersection.

c. Shall be given when it is intended to prohibit all traffic, except pedestrians directed by a pedestrian signal, from entering the intersection or other controlled area.

2. A steady CIRCULAR YELLOW indication:

a. Shall be given following a CIRCULAR GREEN indication in the same signal face.

b. Is an optional alternative to a yellow arrow indication following a green arrow indication in a separate signal face used exclusively to control a single directional movement.

3. A steady CIRCULAR GREEN indication shall be given only when it is intended to permit traffic to proceed in any direction which is lawful and practical.

4. Steady RED ARROW, YELLOW ARROW and GREEN ARROW indications may be used in lieu of the corresponding circular indications at the following locations:

a. On an approach intersecting a one-way street.

b. Where certain movements are prohibited.

c. Where certain movements are physically impossible.

d. On an intersection approach which has an exclusive lane for turning movements.

e. Where turning movements are "protected" from conflicting movements by other indications or by the signal sequence.

f. Where all the movements on the approach do not begin or end at the same time and where the indications for the turning movements will also be visible to traffic with other allowable movements.

If steady arrow indications are used:

a. A steady RED ARROW indication shall be used only in a separate signal face which also contains steady YELLOW ARROW and GREEN ARROW indications. It shall be used for controlling only a single traffic movement.

b. A steady YELLOW ARROW indication shall be used following a GREEN ARROW indication (which has been displayed simultaneously with a CIRCULAR RED indication in the same signal face).

c. A steady YELLOW ARROW indication may be used (in a separate signal face) following a GREEN ARROW indication, when that face is used exclusively to control a single directional movement.

d. A steady YELLOW ARROW indication may be used to indicate the clearance interval following the termination of a GREEN ARROW indication (when displayed simultaneously with a continuing CIRCULAR GREEN indication in the same signal face).

e. A steady GREEN ARROW indication shall be used only when there would be no conflict with other vehicles or with pedestrians crossing in conformance with the WALK indication.

5. The following combinations of signal indications shall not be simultaneously displayed on any one signal face, and shall not be simultaneously displayed in different signal faces on any one approach to an intersection unless the signal faces are shielded, hooded, louvered, positioned or designed so that none of these prohibited combinations of signal indications is readily visible to drivers:

    a. CIRCULAR GREEN with CIRCULAR YELLOW.

    b. Straight-through GREEN ARROW with CIRCULAR RED.

    c. CIRCULAR RED with CIRCULAR YELLOW.

    d. CIRCULAR GREEN with CIRCULAR RED.

    e. CIRCULAR GREEN with RED ARROW.

6. When a traffic control signal is put on flashing operation, normally a yellow indication should be used for the major street and a red indication for the other approaches. Yellow indications shall not be used for all approaches. The following applications shall apply whenever signals are placed in flashing operation:

    a. A CIRCULAR YELLOW indication shall be flashed instead of any YELLOW ARROW indication which may be included in that signal face.

    b. No CIRCULAR GREEN or GREEN ARROW indication or flashing yellow indication shall be terminated and immediately followed by a steady red or flashing red indication without the display of the steady yellow change indication; however, transition may be made directly from a CIRCULAR GREEN or GREEN ARROW indication to a flashing yellow indication.

B-7 Number of Lenses per Signal Face

Each signal face, except in pedestrian signals, shall have at least three lenses, but not more than five. The lenses shall be red, yellow or green in color, and shall give a circular or arrow type of indication. Allowable exceptions to the above are:

1. Where a single section green arrow lens is used alone to indicate a continuous movement.

2. As discussed under Unexpected Conflicts During Green Interval (sec. B-16).

3. Where one or more indications are repeated for reasons of safety or impact.

B-8 Size and Design of Signal Lenses

The aspect of all signal lenses, except in pedestrian signals, shall be circular. There shall be two sizes for lenses, 8 inches and 12 inches nominal diameter.

Twelve-inch lenses normally should be used:

1. For intersections with 85 percentile approach speeds exceeding 40 mph.

2. For intersections where signalization might be unexpected.

3. For special problem locations, such as those with conflicting or competing background lighting.

4. For intersections where drivers may view both traffic control and lane-direction-control signs simultaneously.

5. For all arrow indications.

Arrows shall be pointed vertically upward to indicate a straight-through movement and in a horizontal direction to indicate a turn at approximately right angles. When the angle of the turn is substantially different from a right angle, the arrow should be positioned on an upward slope at an angle approximately equal to that of the turn.

Each arrow lens shall show only one arrow direction. The arrow shall be the only illuminated part of the lens visible.

In no case shall letters or numbers be displayed as part of a vehicular signal indication.

Except for the requirements of this section, all lenses shall conform to the Standard for Adjustable Face Vehicle Traffic Control Signal Heads, 1970 Edition.

B-9 Arrangement of Lenses in Signal Faces

The lenses in a signal face shall be arranged in a vertical or horizontal straight line, except that in a vertical array, lenses of the same color may be arranged horizontally adjacent to each other at right angles to the basic straight line arrangement (fig. 4–1). Such clusters shall be limited to two identical lenses or to two or three different lenses of the same color.

In each signal face, all red lenses in vertical signals shall be located above, and in horizontal signals shall be located to the left of all yellow and green lenses.

A CIRCULAR YELLOW lens shall be located between the red lens or lenses and all other lenses.

In vertically arranged signal faces, each YELLOW ARROW lens shall be located immediately above the GREEN ARROW lens to which it applies. In horizontally arranged signals, the YELLOW ARROW shall be located immediately to the left of the GREEN ARROW lens.

8

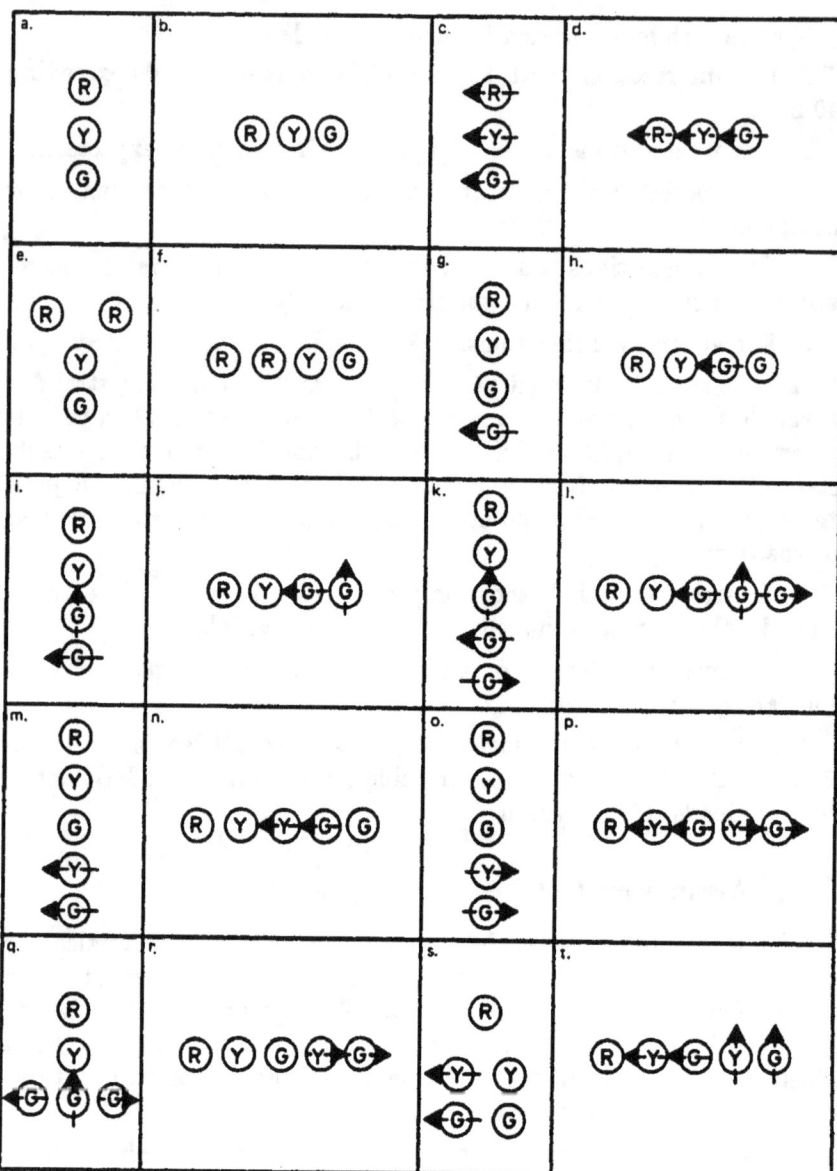

Figure 1. Typical arrangements of lenses in signal faces.

The relative positions of lenses within the signal face shall be as follows:

1. In a vertical signal face from top to bottom:
    CIRCULAR RED
    Left turn RED ARROW
    Right turn RED ARROW
    CIRCULAR YELLOW

Straight through YELLOW ARROW
Straight through GREEN ARROW
CIRCULAR GREEN
Left turn YELLOW ARROW
Left turn GREEN ARROW
Right turn YELLOW ARROW
Right turn GREEN ARROW

2. In a horizontal signal face from left to right:
CIRCULAR RED
Left turn RED ARROW
Right turn RED ARROW
CIRCULAR YELLOW
Left turn YELLOW ARROW
Left turn GREEN ARROW
CIRCULAR GREEN
Straight through YELLOW ARROW
Straight through GREEN ARROW
Right turn YELLOW ARROW
Right turn GREEN ARROW

3. In a cluster, identical signal indications may be repeated in adjacent vertical or horizontal locations within the same signal face. If adjacent indications in a cluster are not identical, their arrangement shall follow paragraph 1 or 2 above, as applicable.

Basic horizontal and vertical display faces may be used on the same approach provided they are separated to meet the lateral clearance required in section B-12.

Figure 1 shows some possible arrangements of lenses in signal faces.

B-10 Illumination of Lenses

Each signal lens shall be illuminated independently.

When a signal lens, except in a pedestrian signal, is illuminated and the view of such an indication is not otherwise physically obstructed, it shall be clearly visible (to drivers it controls) for a distance of a least $\frac{1}{4}$ mile under normal atmospheric conditions.

The intensity and distribution of light from each illuminated signal lens should conform to the Standard for Adjustable Face Vehicle Traffic Control Signal Heads, Revised 1970; and the Standard for Traffic Signal Lamps, December 1967.

When 12" lens signals with 150 watt lamps are placed on flashing for nighttime operation and the flashing yellow indication is so bright as to cause excessive glare, an automatic dimming device should be used to reduce the brilliance of the flashing 12" yellow.

B-11 Visibility and Shielding of Signal Faces

Each signal face shall be so adjusted that its indications will be of maximum effectiveness to the approaching traffic for which they are intended.

Visors should be used on all signal faces to aid in directing the signal indication specifically to approaching traffic, as well as to reduce "sun phantom" resulting from external light entering the lens. Back-plates normally should be used on one-way and back-to-back two-way overhead signals, and when one signal face controls a movement.

In general, vehicular signal faces should be aimed to have maximum effectiveness for an approaching driver located a distance from the stop line equal to the distance traversed while stopping. This distance should include that covered while reacting to the signal as well as that covered while bringing the vehicle to a stop from an average approach speed. The influence of curves, grades, and obstructions should be considered in directing and locating signals.

Irregular street design frequently necessitates placing signals for different street approaches with a comparatively small angle between their indications. In these cases, each signal indication shall, to the extent practicable, be shielded or directed by visors, louvers, or other means so that an approaching driver can see only the indication controlling his movement. Tunnel visors exceeding 12" in length shall not be used on free-swinging signals.

The foregoing does not preclude the use of special signal faces such that the driver does not see their indications before seeing other indications further ahead, when simultaneous viewing of both signal indications could cause the driver to be misdirected.

B-12 Number and Location of Signal Faces

The primary consideration in signal face placement shall be visibility. Drivers approaching a signalized intersection or other signalized area, such as a mid-block crosswalk, shall be given a clear and unmistakable indication of their right-of-way assignment. Critical elements are lateral and vertical angles of sight toward a signal face, as determined by typical driver eye position, vehicle design, and the vertical, longitudinal and lateral position of the signal face. The geometry of each intersection to be signalized, including vertical grades and horizontal curves, should be considered in signal face placement.

The visibility, location and number of signal faces for each approach to an intersection or a mid-block crosswalk shall be as follows:

1. A minimum of two signal faces for through-traffic shall be provided and should be continuously visible from a point at least the following distances in advance of and to the stop line, unless physical obstruction of their visibility exists:

85 Percentile Speed	Minimum Visibility Distance (Ft.)
20	100
25	175
30	250
35	325
40	400
45	475
50	550
55	625
60	700

2. Where physical conditions prevent drivers from having a continuous view of at least two signal indications as specified herein, a suitable sign shall be erected to warn approaching traffic. It may be supplemented by a Hazard Identification Beacon.
A beacon utilized in this manner may be interconnected with the traffic signal controller in such a manner as to flash yellow during the period when drivers passing this beacon, at the legal speed for the roadway, may encounter a red signal upon arrival at the signalized location.

3. A single signal face is permissible for the control of an exclusive turn lane. Such a signal face shall be in addition to the minimum of two signal faces for through-traffic. When the indications of a separate signal face or faces controlling an exclusive turn lane will also be visible to traffic with other allowable movements, a sign LEFT (or RIGHT) TURN SIGNAL shall be located adjacent to such signal face. When the face consists entirely of arrow indications, such a sign is not required.

4. Except where the width of the intersecting street or other conditions make it physically impractical, at least one and preferably both of the signal faces required by paragraph (1) above shall be located not less than 40 feet nor more than 120 feet beyond the stop line. Where both of the signal faces required by paragraph (1) above are post-mounted, they shall both be on the far side of the intersection, one on the right and one on the left or on the median island if practical. The signal face required by paragraph (3) above shall conform to the same location requirements as the signal faces required by paragraph (1) to the extent practical.

5. Except where the width of the intersecting street or other conditions make it physically impractical, at least one and preferably

both of the signal faces required by paragraph (1) above shall be located between two lines intersecting with the center of the approach lanes at the stop line, one making an angle of approximately 20 degrees to the right of the center of the approach extended, and the other making an angle of approximately 20 degrees to the left of the center of the approach extended (fig. 2).

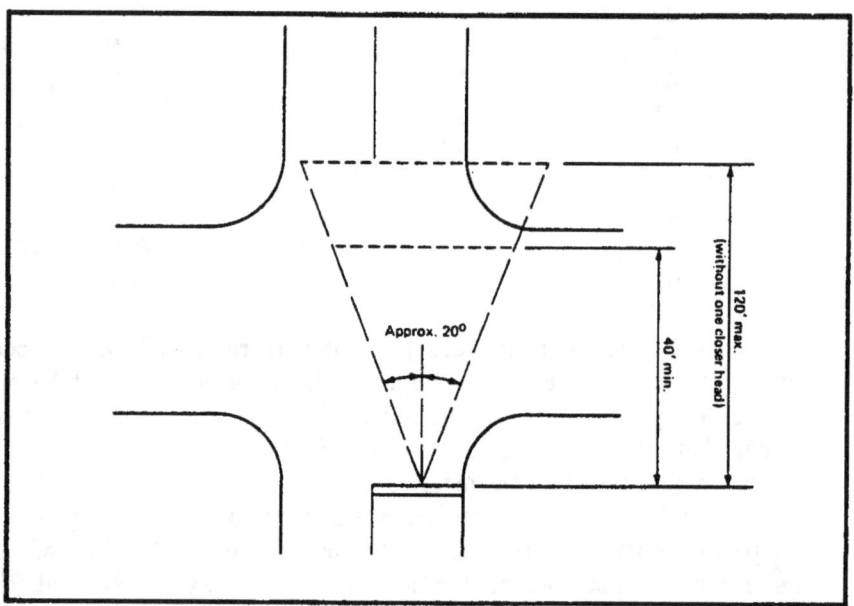

Figure 2. Desirable location of signal faces.

6. Near-side signals should be located as near as practicable to the stop line.

7. Where a signal face controls a specific lane or lanes of approach, its transverse position should be unmistakably in line with the path of that movement.

8. Required signal faces for any one approach shall be not less than eight feet apart measured horizontally between centers of faces.

9. When the nearest signal face is more than 120 feet beyond the stop line, a supplemental near side signal indication shall be provided.

10. A signal face mounted on a span wire or mast arm should be located as near as practicable to the line of the driver's normal view.

11. Supplemental signal faces should be used when an engineering study has shown that they are needed to achieve both advance and immediate intersection visibility. When used, they should be lo-

cated to provide optimum visibility for the movement to be controlled. The following limitations apply:

    a. Left turn arrows shall not be used in near-right faces.

    b. Right turn arrows shall not be used in far-left faces. A far-side median mount signal shall be considered as a far-left signal for this application.

At signalized mid-block crosswalks, there should be at least one signal face over the traveled roadway for each approach. In other respects, a traffic control signal at a mid-block location shall meet the requirements set forth herein.

The transverse location of a signal face, shall, if mounted on the top of a post or on a short bracket from it, conform with section B–14.

Supplementary pedestrian signals shall be used where warranted,

B–13 Height of Signal Faces

The bottom of the housing of a signal face, not mounted over a roadway, shall not be less than 8 feet nor more than 15 feet above the sidewalk or, if none, above the pavement grade at the center of the highway.

The bottom of the housing of a signal face suspended over a roadway shall not be less than 15 feet nor more than 19 feet above the pavement grade at the center of the roadway.

Within the above limits, optimum visibility and adequate clearance should be the guiding considerations in deciding signal height. Grades on approaching streets may be important factors, and should be considered in determining the most appropriate height.

B–14 Transverse Location of Traffic Signal Supports and Controller Cabinets

In the placement of signal supports, primary consideration shall be given to ensuring the proper visibility of signal faces as described in sections B–12 and 13. However, in the interest of safety, signal supports and controller cabinets should be placed as far as practicable from the edge of the traveled way without adversely affecting signal visibility.

Supports for post-mounted signal heads at the side of a street with curbs shall have a horizontal clearance of not less than two feet from the face of a vertical curb. Where there is no curb, supports for post-mounted signal heads shall have a horizontal clearance of not less than two feet from the edge of a shoulder, within the limits of normal vertical clearance. A signal support should not obstruct a crosswalk.

No part of a concrete base for a signal support should extend more than 4 inches above the ground level at any point, except that this limitation does not apply to the concrete base for a rigid (non-breakaway) support.

On medians, the above minimum clearances for signal supports should be obtained where practicable. Any supports which cannot be located with the required clearances should be of the breakaway type or should be guarded if at all practicable.

B-15 Vehicle Change Interval

A yellow vehicle change interval shall be used following each CIRCULAR GREEN interval and, where applicable after each GREEN ARROW interval. In no case shall a CIRCULAR YELLOW indication be displayed in conjunction with the change from CIRCULAR RED to CIRCULAR GREEN. Separate signal faces should be used when exclusive turning movements are controlled by GREEN ARROWS (sec. B-6).

The exclusive function of the steady yellow interval shall be to warn traffic of an impending change in the right-of-way assignment.

Yellow vehicle change intervals should have a range of approximately 3 to 6 seconds. Generally the longer intervals are appropriate to higher approach speeds.

The yellow vehicle change interval may be followed by a short all-way red clearance interval, of sufficient duration to permit the intersection to clear before cross traffic is released.

A clearance interval shall be provided between the termination of a GREEN ARROW indication and the showing of a green indication to any conflicting traffic movement.

B-16 Unexpected Conflicts During Green Interval

No movement that may involve an unexpected crossing of pathways of moving traffic should be indicated during any green interval, except when:

1. The movement involves only slight hazard;
2. Serious traffic delays are materially reduced by permitting the conflicting movement; and
3. Drivers and pedestrians subjected to the unexpected conflict are effectively warned thereof.

When such conditions of possible unexpected conflict exist, warning may be given by a sign or, by the use of an appropriate signal indication as set forth in section B-7. The foregoing applies to vehicle-pedestrian conflicts as well as to vehicle-vehicle conflicts.

B-17 Coordination of Traffic Control Signals

Traffic control signals within one-half of a mile of one another along a major route or in a network of intersecting major routes should be operated in coordination, preferably with interconnected controllers. However, coordination need not be maintained across boundaries between signal systems which operate on different time cycles. Coordinated operation normally should include both pre-timed signals and traffic-actuated signals within the appropriate distances.

For coordination with railroad grade crossings signals see section B-21.

B-18 Flashing Operation of Traffic Control Signals

All traffic signal installations shall be provided with an electrical flashing mechanism supplementary to the signal timer. A manual switch, or where appropriate, automatic means, shall be provided to actuate the flashing mechanism. The signal timer shall be removable without affecting the flashing operation. The mechanism shall operate in a manner similar to that of an Intersection Control Beacon to provide intermittent illumination of selected signal lenses.

The illuminating element in a flashing signal shall be flashed continuously at a rate of not less than 50 nor more than 60 times per minute. The illuminated period of each flash shall be not less than half and not more than two-thirds of the total flash cycle.

When traffic control signals are put on flashing operation, the signal indications given to the several streets shall be as specified in section B-6.

Automatic changes from flashing to stop-and-go operation shall be made at the beginning of the major street green interval, preferably at the beginning of the common major street green interval, (i.e., when a green indication is shown in both directions on the major street). Automatic changes from stop-and-go to flashing operation shall be made at the end of the common major street red interval, (i.e., when a red indication is shown in both directions on the major street).

The change from the flashing to stop-and-go operation, or from stop-and-go to flashing operation by manual switch may be made at any time.

Where there is no common major street green interval, the automatic change from flashing to stop-and-go operation shall be made at the beginning of the green interval for the major traffic movement on the major street. It may be necessary to provide a short, steady all-red interval for the other approaches before changing from flashing yellow or flashing red to green on the major approach.

B-19 Continuity of Operation

A traffic signal installation, except as provided below, shall be operated as a stop-and-go device or as a flashing device.

When a signal installation is not in operation such as prior to placing it in service, during seasonal shutdowns, or when it is not desirable to operate the signals, they should be hooded, turned or taken down to clearly indicate that the signal is not in operation.

When a traffic signal installation is being operated in the usual (stop-and-go) manner, at least one indication in each signal face shall be illuminated.

When a traffic signal installation is being operated as a flashing device, the yellow indication shall be flashed in at least two required signal faces (sec. B–12) on each approach on which traffic is not stopped and the red indication shall be flashed in at least two required signal faces (sec. B–12) on each approach on which traffic is required to stop.

The above provisions do not apply to emergency-traffic signals or draw-bridge signals.

When a single-section, continuously illuminated GREEN ARROW lens is used alone to indicate a continuous movement, it may be continuously illuminated when the other signal indications in the signal installation are flashed.

B-20 Signal Operation Must Relate to Traffic Flow

Traffic control signals shall be operated in a manner consistent with traffic requirements. Data from engineering studies shall be used to determine the proper phasing and timing for a signal.

Since traffic flows and patterns change, it is necessary that the engineering data be updated and re-evaluated regularly.

To assure that the approved operating pattern including timing is displayed to the driver, regular checks including the use of accurate timing devices should be made.

B-21 Traffic Signals Near Grade Crossings

When a railroad grade crossing, protected by train-approach signals is within or near an intersection controlled by a traffic control signal, the control of the traffic signal should be preempted from the signal controller upon approach of trains to avoid conflicting aspects of the traffic signal and the train-approach signal. This preemption feature requires a closed electrical circuit between the control relay of the train-approach signals and the preemptor in order to establish and maintain the preempted condition during the time that the train-approach signals are in operation. Except under unusual circumstances, the interconnection should be limited to the traffic signals within 200 feet of the crossing.

Traffic control signals shall not be used on mainline railroad crossings in lieu of railroad grade crossing protection devices. However, at industrial track crossings and other places where train movements are very slow (as in switching operations), traffic control signals may be used in lieu of conventional train-approach signals to warn motorists of the approach or presence of a train. The provisions of this part relating to traffic signal design, installation and operation are applicable as appropriate where traffic control signals are so used.

At crossings where train movements are regulated or limited to the extent that train-approach signals are not required, preemption of the adjacent signalized intersections may be desirable to permit non-conflicting highway traffic to proceed during the time the crossing is blocked by a train. Except under unusual circumstances, the interconnection should be limited to the traffic signals within 200 feet of the crossing.

The preemption sequence initiated when the train first enters the approach circuit, shall at once bring into effect a signal display which will permit all vehicles to clear the tracks before the train reaches the intersection or any approach thereto.

When the green indication is preempted by train operation, a yellow change interval must be inserted in the signal sequence in the interest of safety and consistency. To avoid misinterpretation during the time that the clear-out signals are green, consideration should be given to the use of 12-inch red lenses in the signals which govern movement over the tracks (sec. B-8).

After the track clearance phase, the traffic control signal may be operated to permit vehicle movements that do not cross the tracks, but in all cases shall prohibit movements over the tracks.

Where feasible the location and the normal (no trains involved) phasing and timing of traffic control signals near railroad grade crossings should be designed so that vehicles are not required to stop on the tracks even though in some cases this will increase the waiting time. The exact nature of the display and the location of the signals to accomplish this will depend on the physical relationship of the tracks to the intersection area.

When the train clears the crossing it is necessary to return the signal to a designated phase, normally the traffic movement crossing the tracks.

As used herein, the terms "train" and "railroad" shall include transit vehicles operating upon stationary rails or tracks on private right-of-way.

B-22 Emergency Operation of Traffic Signals

Systems in which traffic control signals are preempted by emergency vehicles shall operate to permit a normal change interval to take place in the change from green to yellow to red (or flashing red) before arrival of the emergency vehicle at the preempted location. Systems in which traffic control signals are preempted by emergency vehicles shall be designed and installed so as to provide an indication to the driver of any emergency vehicle approaching an intersection when the equipment fails to preempt the traffic signal at that intersection. This indication shall be designed to be given whether the failure results from a prior preemption by an emergency vehicle on the cross street, by a railroad preemption, from equipment malfunction, or from any other cause.

Traffic signals operating in congested areas during emergency conditions should be operated in a manner designed to keep traffic moving. Prolonged all-red or flashing signal sequences are to be avoided.

B-23 Maintenance of Traffic Control Signals

Prior to the installation of any traffic control signal, the responsibility for its maintenance should be clearly established. The responsible agency should provide for the maintenance of the signal and all of its appurtenances in a responsible manner. To this end the agency should:

1. Provide for alternate operation of the signal during a period of failure, either on flash or manually, or by having manual traffic direction by proper authority as may be warranted by traffic volumes or congestion, or by erecting other traffic control devices.
2. Have properly skilled maintenance available without undue delay for all emergency calls, including lamp failures.
3. Provide properly skilled maintenance for all components.
4. Maintain the appearance of the installation in a manner consistent with the intention of this part, with particular emphasis on painting and on cleaning of the optical system.
5. Service equipment and lamps as frequently as experience proves necessary to prevent undue failures.
6. Provide adequate stand-by equipment to minimize the interruption of signal operation due to equipment failure.

Every controller should be kept in effective operation in strict accordance with its predetermined timing schedule.

A careful check of the correctness of time operation of the controller should be made frequently enough to insure its operating in accordance with the planned timing schedule. Timing changes should be made only by authorized persons. A written record should be made of all timing changes.

Controllers should be carefully cleaned and serviced at least as frequently as specified by the manufacturer and more frequently if experience proves it necessary.

B-24 Painting

The insides of visors (hoods) and the entire surface of louvers, and fins, and the front surface of backplates shall have a dull black finish to minimize light reflection to the side of the signals.

To obtain the best possible contrast with the visual background, it is desirable to paint signal head housings highway yellow.

B-25 Vehicle Detectors

The placement of vehicle detectors in relation to the Stop line is a very important factor in the proper operation of traffic actuated signals and should be a factor in signal design.

Where the total entering traffic on one street is more than twice that on the cross street, detectors on the cross street should be placed closer to the stop line than on the main street.

Additional "calling" detectors may be required on lower volume streets to handle traffic entering the street from driveways between the basic detector and the Stop line.

The transverse placement of detectors should be such that vehicles traveling away from the intersection do not register "false-calls." On narrow two-way roadways this may require use of directional detectors.

B-26 Auxiliary Signs

Signal instruction signs used with traffic signals shall be located adjacent to the signal face to which they apply. Minimum clearance of the total assembly shall conform to the provisions of sections A-23 and B-13.

Stop signs shall not be used in conjunction with any signal operation, except:

1. When the indication flashes red at all times or
2. When a minor street or driveway is located within or adjacent to the controlled area, but does not warrant separate signal control due to extremely low potential for conflict.

When used in conjunction with traffic signals, illuminated signs shall be designed and mounted in such a manner as to avoid glare and reflections that seriously detract from the signal indications. The traffic control signal shall be given dominant position and brightness to assure its target priority in the overall display.

Traffic Signal Speed signs may be used to inform drivers of the speed of progression, if this speed is substantially lower than the speed limits in effect on streets in the signal system.

B-27 Removal of Confusing Advertising Lights

There should be legal authority to prohibit the display of any unauthorized sign, signal, marking, or device which interferes with the effectiveness of any official traffic control device. Specific reference is made to Section 11-205, Uniform Vehicle Code—Revised 1968.

TRAFFIC ENGINEERING

BASIC FUNDAMENTALS OF TRAFFIC PLANNING

CONTENTS

	Page
CHAPTER 1 – CONCEPT	1-1
CHAPTER 2 – ORGANIZATION	2-1
CHAPTER 3 – PROCESS	3-1

Basic Fundamentals of Traffic Planning

THOROUGHFARE PLANNING *is a method of identifying travel needs and filling them — to make road travel safe, economical, convenient, free-flowing, and environmentally acceptable.* Thoroughfare planners insure that roadways will accommodate traffic demands, maximize the use of roadways, and solve traffic problems.

THOROUGHFARE PLANNING *provides not only for modifications to existing roadways to meet current traffic demands; it provides also for the identification of land areas that should be reserved for roadway expansion to meet future traffic demands.* Planners, working toward established goals, may recommend that a particular street be retained or redesigned as necessary to perform a specific function. **Effective thoroughfare planning can reap savings in construction and maintenance costs, protect housing areas, and control travel and land-use patterns.**

CONCEPT

PLANNING IS A STEP-BY-STEP PROCESS

The **planning process** is a method to:

Identify problems and establish goals and objectives.

Conduct traffic surveys, analyze the survey data, and estimate future traffic volumes and patterns.

Develop alternate solutions and test them against the goals and objectives, then select and implement a final plan.

Review and evaluate the plan on a continuing basis and adjust it as necessary to attain desired goals and objectives.

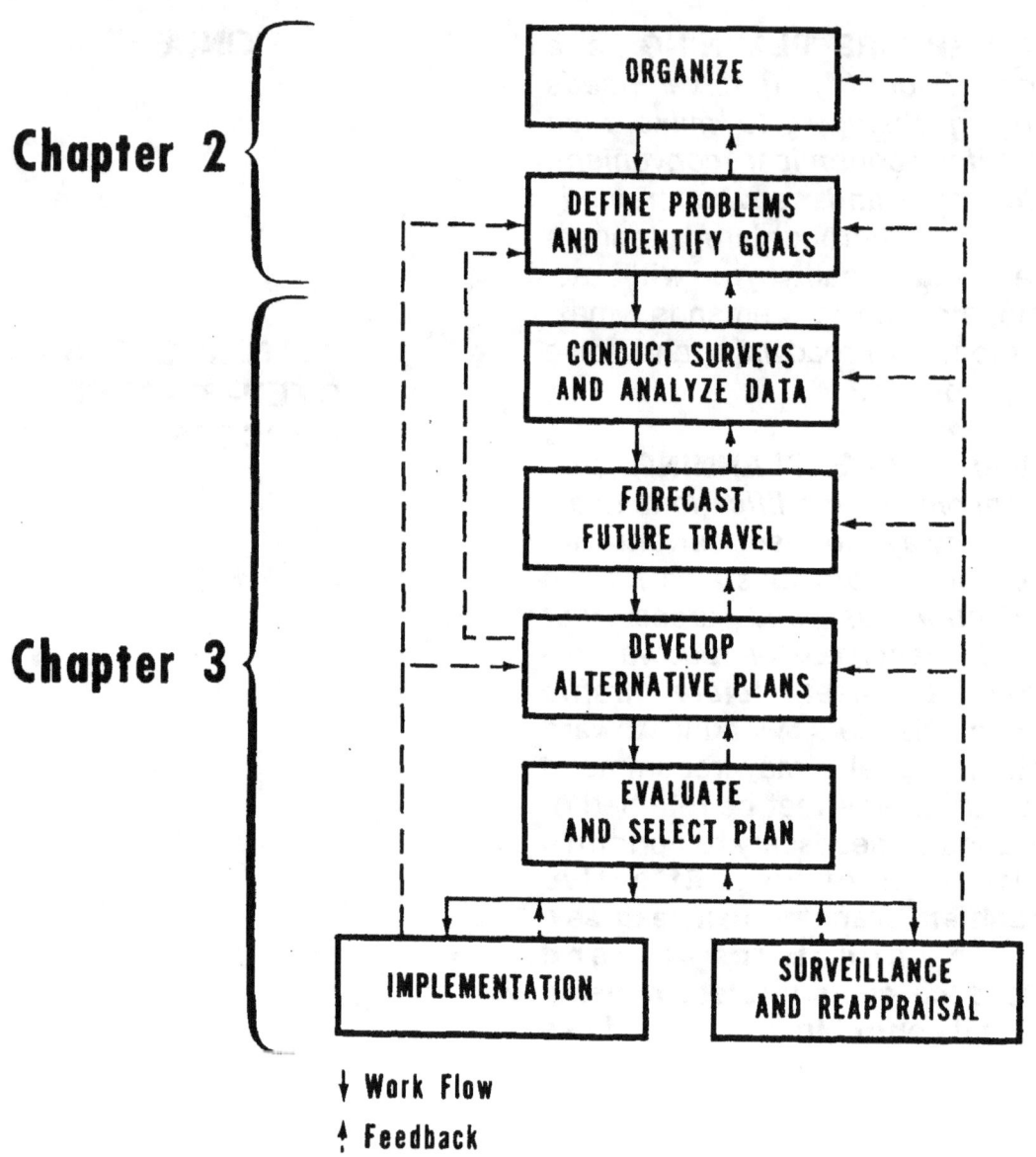

A step-by-step discussion of the planning process is presented in Chapters 2 and 3. Chapter 2 discusses the prerequisites to effective and continuing planning — that is, the formation of a planning committee, the identification of problems, and the establishment of goals. Chapter 3 summarizes the remaining steps to be taken to develop alternative plans for evaluation, selection, and implementation.

ORGANIZATION

PLANNING COMMITTEE

PROBLEM DEFINITION AND GOAL IDENTIFICATION

TRAFFIC PLANNING GOALS must be **determined by the installation decisionmakers,** with the **assistance of technical experts.** Technical experts should provide direction for the decisionmakers *through rational analysis of installation needs and policies.* With this information, **decisionmakers** can effectively select goals and a planning program that will insure an end product that is both workable and desirable.

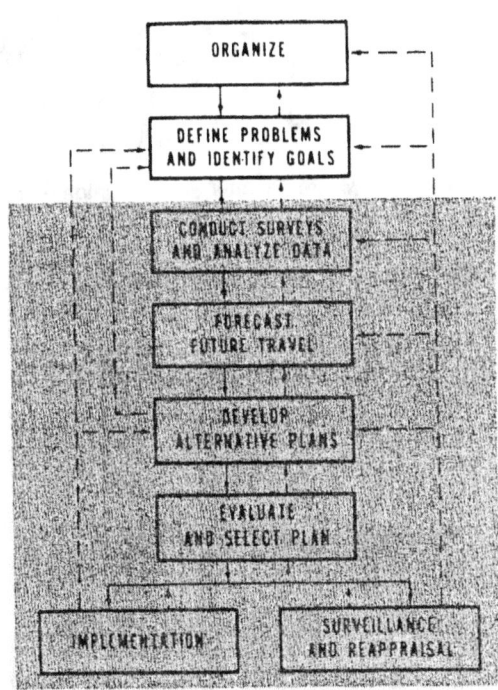

PLANNING COMMITTEE

EFFECTIVE THOROUGHFARE PLANNING *requires concerted effort among policymakers and the technical and administrative staffs of the installation under study.* Each step of the planning process must be based on a simple framework in which the installation's decisionmakers can clearly understand not only the traffic problems, but also the solution to those problems. Committee members usually should be selected to represent the installation's diverse disciplines and viewpoints. For example, an individual representing each of the groups shown below would be desirable.

DECISIONMAKERS MUST

- Identify Traffic Problems
- Establish Goals to Reduce Problems
- Select Thoroughfare Plan
- Gain Support for Plan

TECHNICAL STAFF MUST

- Conduct Traffic Studies
- Estimate Future Travel
- Develop Alternate Plans
- Implement Plan

PROBLEM DEFINITION AND GOAL IDENTIFICATION

THE FIRST STEP IN THOROUGHFARE PLANNING is to **clearly identify all traffic problems of the installation** being studied.

The term *"traffic problem"* is defined as *any situation that impairs the safe and efficient flow of traffic.*

In identifying traffic problems, relativity must be considered; that is, traffic problems vary among different areas of the country. For example, a 5-minute delay in New York City is considered as negligible, while the same delay in Timbuktu would be extremely frustrating to motorists. Therefore, it must be remembered that **traffic problems are relative to the installation being studied.**

FOR EVERY TRAFFIC PROBLEM, THERE IS A POSITIVE GOAL

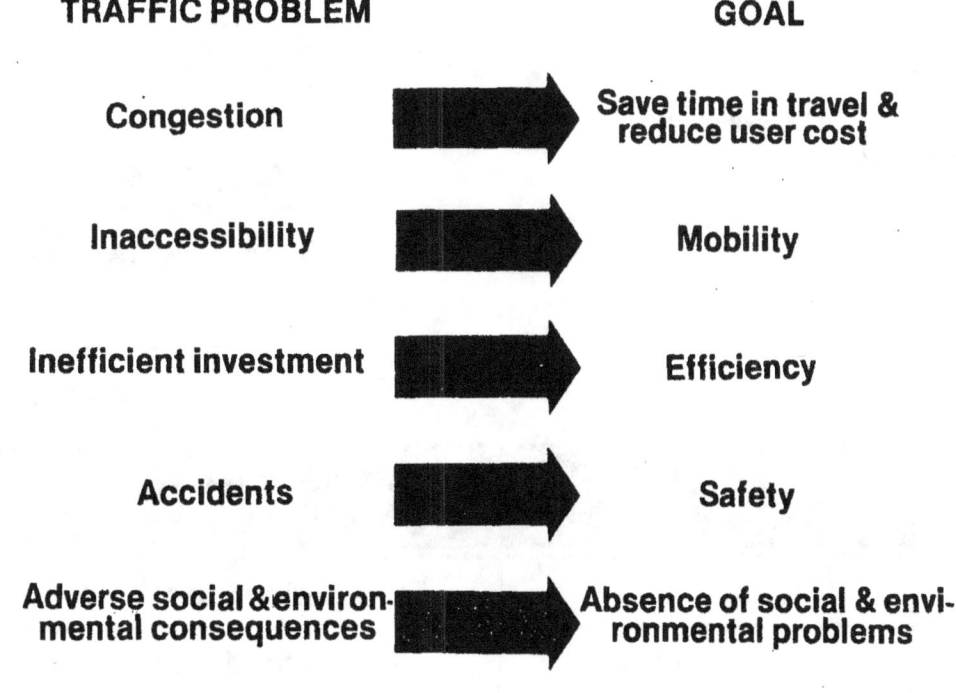

TRAFFIC PROBLEM	GOAL
Congestion	Save time in travel & reduce user cost
Inaccessibility	Mobility
Inefficient investment	Efficiency
Accidents	Safety
Adverse social & environmental consequences	Absence of social & environmental problems

101

2-4

PROBLEM:

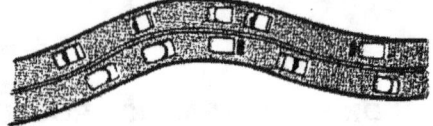

CONGESTION wastes time and increases operating costs.

CONGESTION — Motorists dislike traffic congestion primarily because of wasted time and the resulting increased operating costs. Excessive operating costs can be measured with a fair degree of precision. For example, on a 1-mile free-flowing roadway of 30 miles-per-hour speed, three stops of 30-seconds duration each will result in an increase of approximately 90 percent in total running cost of the car. Measuring the value of a motorist's time is far more difficult. However, evidence shows that, given a choice, motorists will forfeit operating economy to save time.

GOAL: TO PROVIDE EFFICIENT TRAFFIC FLOW

ADEQUATE CAPACITY saves time and reduces operating cost.

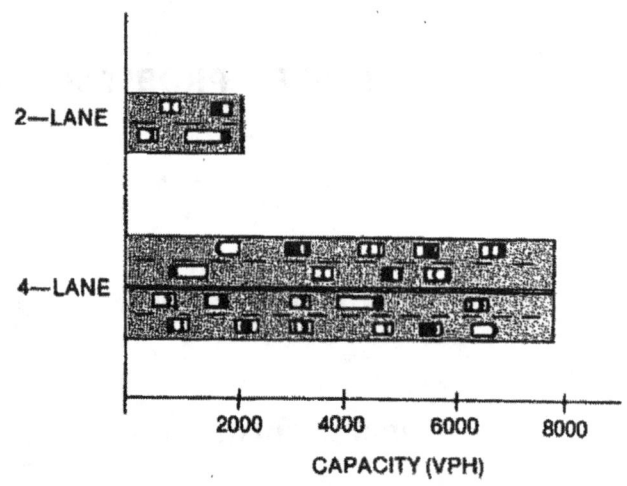

OBJECTIVE	INDICATOR
Cut travel time	Peak period travel time
Minimize congestion	Peak period volume
Reduce user cost	Vehicle user cost

PROBLEM:

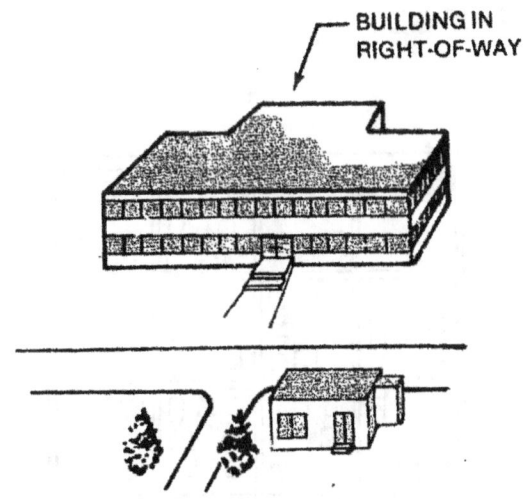

INACCESSIBILITY — Most people like to have the freedom to get where they want to go, when they want to go. High productivity is closely related to proximity in time. Without access, land cannot be developed and people cannot move to jobs, schools, hospitals, and so forth.

GOAL: TO IMPROVE MOBILITY OF POPULATION

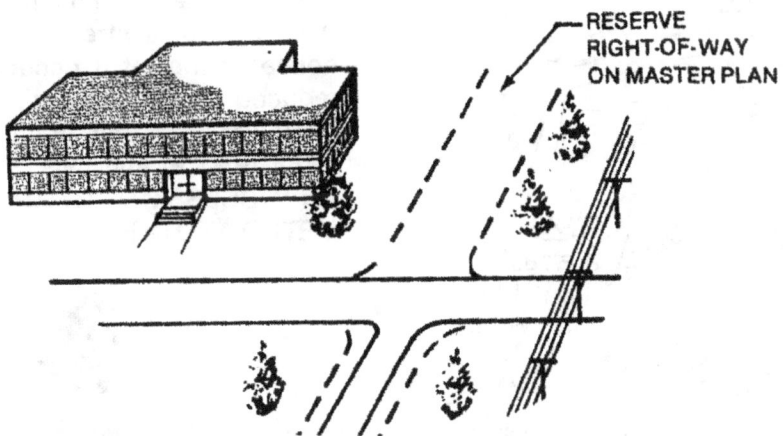

OBJECTIVE	INDICATOR
Reduce travel distance	Distance between point A and point B
Increase productivity of land and people	Changes in access caused by land development

PROBLEM:

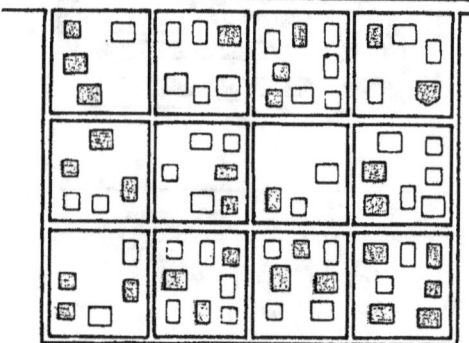

Where width of street, size of house, or size of lot is squeezed to a so-called "efficient minimum" — this is false economy.

INEFFICIENT INVESTMENT — Another universally condemned action is waste of public funds. The case of building unusable traffic facilities or misappropriating public funds is quite rare. However, the more frequent and important waste is that of false economy in traffic facilities. For example, decisions on expenditure are generally based on their budget appeal, not on their adequacy, such as patchwork improvements. The question of whether improvements may solve any particular problem is usually overlooked or avoided; example, a street-widening may prove inadequate the day it is completed and require immediate improvements. Another type of false economy results from so-called "efficient" planning, which creates waste. For example, in housing areas where the width of a street or the size of a house or the lot it occupies has been reduced to a so-called "efficient minimum" — this is false economy. EFFICIENT PLANNING IS MORE THAN AN OBSESSION TO SAVE; IT IS A METHOD TO IMPROVE.

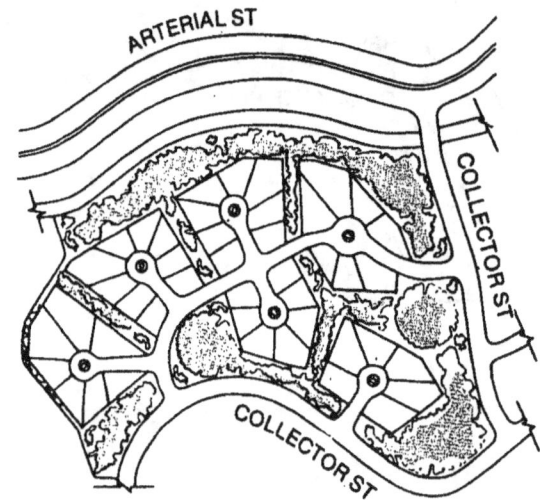

A modern residential street design preserves the neighborhood.

GOAL: TO ELIMINATE WASTE OF PUBLIC FUNDS AND PROTECT LIFE STYLE PATTERNS.

OBJECTIVE	INDICATOR
Decide expenditures based on adequacy, NOT budget appeal	Existing and desirable life-style patterns

PROBLEM:

ACCIDENTS — Accidents are the most significant of all traffic problems. In 1975 alone, approximately 58,800 motor vehicle accidents occurred on military installations, and resulted in an estimated cost of $70,000,000 to DOD and its personnel. Recent surveys of military installations revealed that the yearly accident rate ranged from 1 to over 40 per 1,000 people. This wide range indicates that the accident rate of an installation can be reduced through better traffic facilities.

ACCIDENT COST TO DOD
FATALITY — $287,175 per accident
PERSONAL INJURY — $8,085 per accident
PROPERTY DAMAGE — $520 per accident

GOAL: TO PROVIDE SAFE TRAVEL ROAD

FOUR-LANE UNDIVIDED

VERSUS

4.09 accidents per million vehicle miles

FOUR-LANE DIVIDED

2.91 accidents per million vehicle miles

The reduction of accidents on a four-lane divided highway is 29% over the undivided highway

OBJECTIVE	INDICATOR
Reduce accidents and fatalities	Number of accidents and fatalities

PROBLEM:

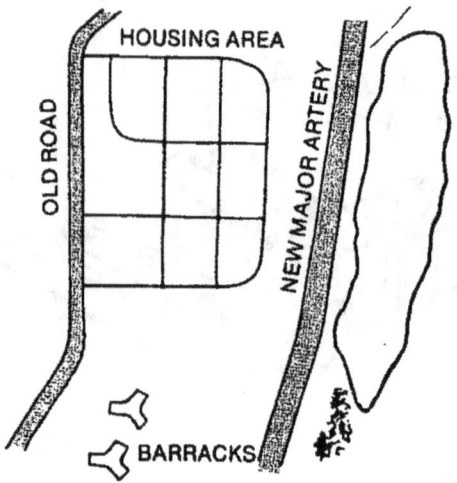

Noise Pollution.

SOCIAL AND ENVIRONMENTAL IMPACT — Ugliness, air pollution, strain, discomfort, noise, and nuisance are all components of the increasingly social nature of transportation problems. All of these problems are difficult to measure. Furthermore, problems such as ugliness are visual images that vary markedly among people, and hence it is difficult to obtain a consensus. The best way to consider these problems is in final plan selection.

GOAL: TO ENHANCE ENVIRONMENT

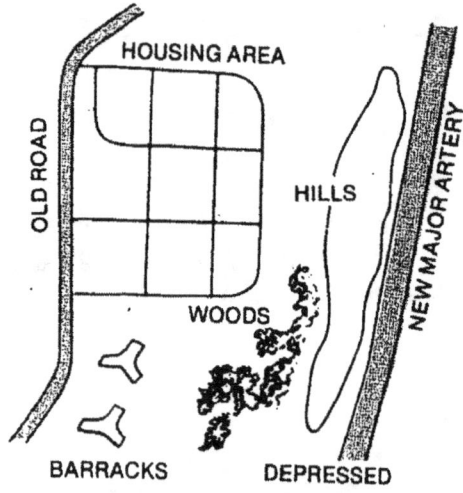

Built-In Noise Protection and Abatement

OBJECTIVE	INDICATOR
Minimize air/noise pollution	Exposure to pollution
Preserve open space	Recreational land available
Reduce travel on residential streets	Traffic volume on streets
Enhance views	Subjective judgment

2-9

BE AWARE OF CONFLICTS BETWEEN GOALS

Simply having an agreed set of goals and objectives is not enough because of the conflicts between goals. For example, the least expensive, initially, is to do nothing; whereas, the safest could very likely be the most expensive. Basically, goals should be listed and then screened to eliminate all but the most relevant. The goals selected should then be related to each other, so that losses toward one goal could be offset by gains toward another. Finally, these goals should be related to minimizing the total transportation costs.

III. PROCESS

SURVEYS

FORECAST

DEVELOPMENT

EVALUATION

IMPLEMENTATION

SURVEILLANCE AND REAPPRAISAL

THE ESTABLISHMENT OF A PLANNING PROCEDURE *is necessary in drafting a thoroughfare plan.* The process begins with **a review of existing facilities and travel characteristics. Data for present conditions** are then projected to the design year, and future deficiencies are noted. Based on these projections, **alternative improvements to present conditions** are evaluated, **a general thoroughfare plan** is selected, and **a priority schedule** is developed for implementation. The previous steps are continually reevaluated in view of the data developed at each succeeding step.

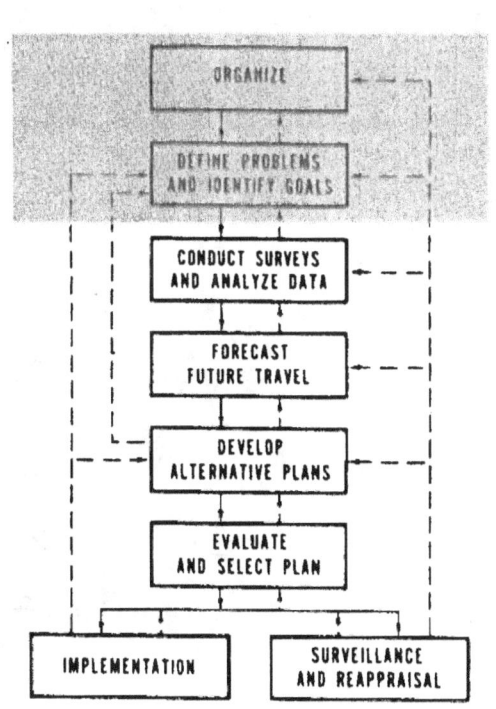

The cornerstone of the thoroughfare plan is the existing street system. Today's adequate street system, when projected to the design year, may become inadequate. The thoroughfare plan should lead to a design that will efficiently handle traffic volumes of the average weekday peak-traffic hours for the design year. These peak-hour flows usually are highly directional, with heavy inbound traffic in the morning and heavy outbound traffic in the evening. Occasionally, other time periods will determine a design for community service and retail-facility areas.

SURVEYS

SURVEYS are conducted to gather data on the present condition and traffic characteristics of an installation's roadways. These **data** are **analyzed** to estimate the traffic demands on the roadways and, as necessary, to redesign, evaluate, and program a road system to meet those demands.

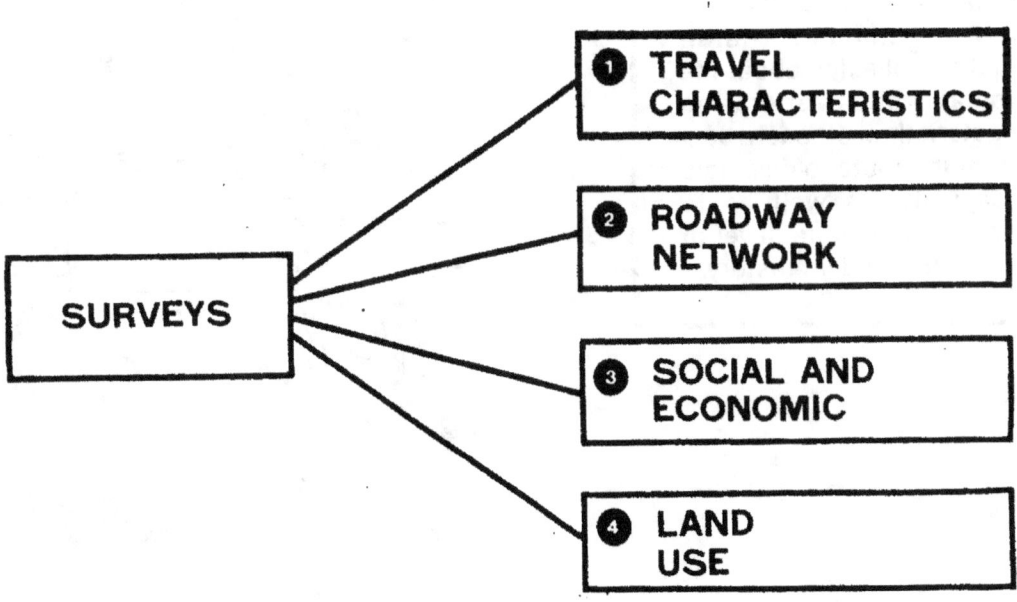

3-4

1. TRAVEL CHARACTERISTICS

These surveys determine how many people use the road system, who they are, and their travel patterns. Data are gathered primarily from studies on traffic volume, vehicle occupancy, travel time and delay, and trip origin and destination. Of major interest to the installation thoroughfare planner is the employee home-to-work trip.

ESTABLISHES ROAD USAGE

2. ROAD NETWORK

These surveys determine the condition and capacity of the roadway. Enough detail should be collected about the physical and operating characteristics of each segment of the route to calculate its capacity, as well as to determine its general level of service and accident history.

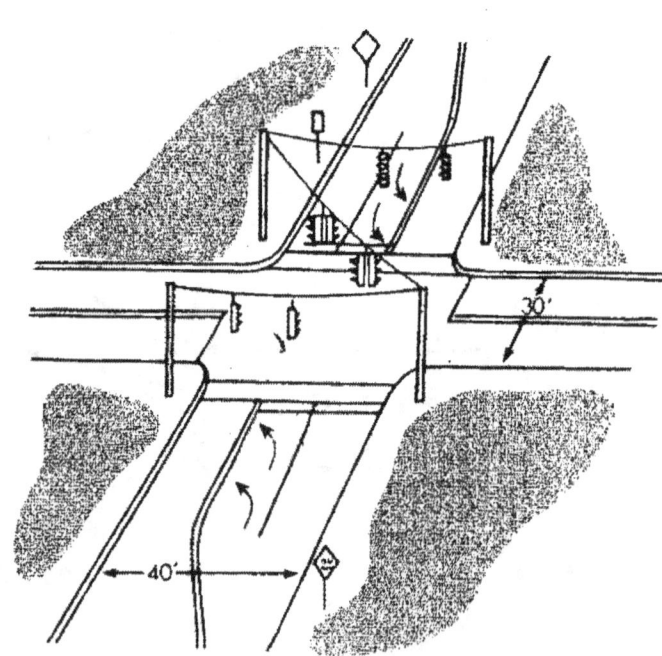

ESTABLISHES ROAD CONDITIONS

3 SOCIAL AND ECONOMIC

These surveys establish past and present facts about the installation road user. Typical data collected include population, employment, duty hours, housing, social services, security measures, and carpool programs. These data are used primarily as a basis for forecasting growth potential. The data are used also for origin and destination surveys and as variables to determine trip generations.

ESTABLISHES ROAD USER CHARACTERISTICS

4 LAND USE

Land patterns delineate the function of the land and are basic factors in determining traffic demands of an installation.

A simplified land-use classification system should include at least five categories:

RESIDENTIAL — single-family housing, apartment housing, bachelor officer and enlisted quarters.

ADMINISTRATIVE AND COMMERCIAL — offices, training centers, and exchanges.

INDUSTRIAL AND OPERATIONAL — maintenance and production facilities, ranges, motorpools, airports, and waterfront facilities.

COMMUNITY SERVICE — dependent schools, parks, churches, and recreational facilities.

OPEN SPACE — undeveloped acreage, forest, and streams.

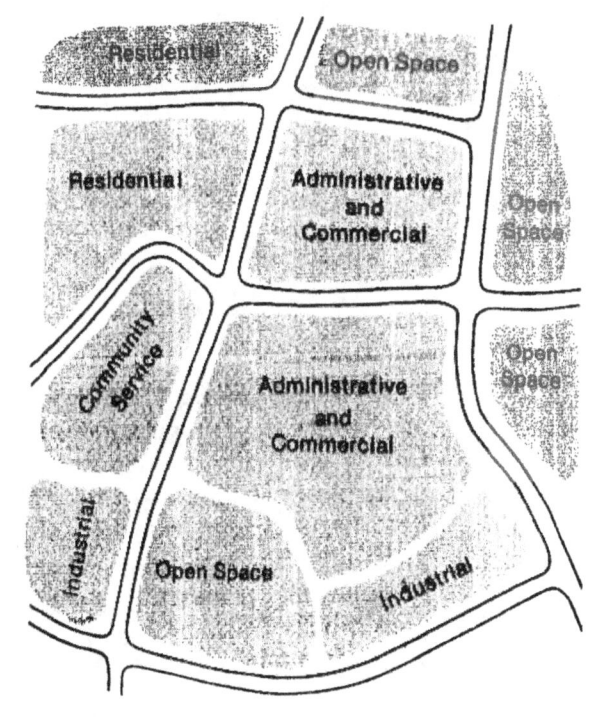

DELINEATES LAND FUNCTION

FORECAST

TRAVEL FORECASTS *are used to determine the transportation service NEED that will result from a change in land use.* For example, what roads will be needed to service a new housing area. Travel forecasts can include home-based, nonhome-based, work, nonwork, person, vehicle, and other type trips. Therefore, **the key to reducing the complexity of a travel forecast** *is to limit the forecast to only what is NEEDED to establish the maximum travel demand.* At a military installation, maximum travel demand is generally created by the highly directional employee home-to-work vehicle-trip that occurs during the morning or evening peak rush hour. Travel forecasts often need to establish only this type demand. A notable exception to this criterion is facilities that generate large traffic volumes not associated with the work trip, such as commercial and community facilities.

TRAVEL FORECASTS QUANTIFY FUTURE TRAFFIC DEMAND

THE FORECAST PROCESS starts with the **proposed road network and land use,** along with a **thorough understanding of existing traffic flow patterns.** Based on this information, **a prediction** is made of the number of future trips to and from an activity **(trip generation),** where these trips begin and end **(trip distribution),** and over which routes the trips are to be made **(trip assignment).** This process is then used to **evaluate** various alternative road systems. After each numerical evaluation, all forecasts are examined to determine if they are reasonable. If the forecast is unreasonable, the assumptions and procedures used to predict the trips should be reexamined and appropriate changes made.

SURVEYS
Existing Conditions

① LAND USE
Where will activities and roads be located?

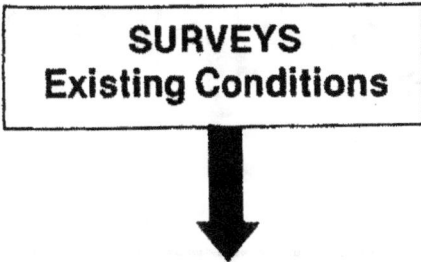

② TRIP GENERATION*
How many trips begin and end at the activity?

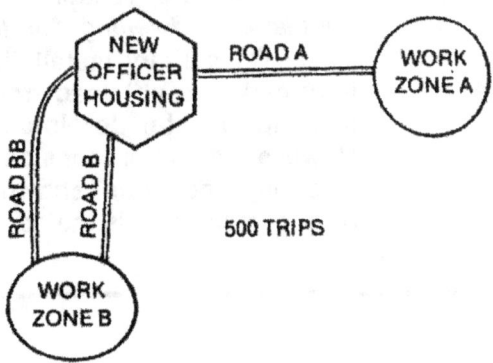

500 TRIPS

③ TRIP DISTRIBUTION*
How many trips will be made between activities?

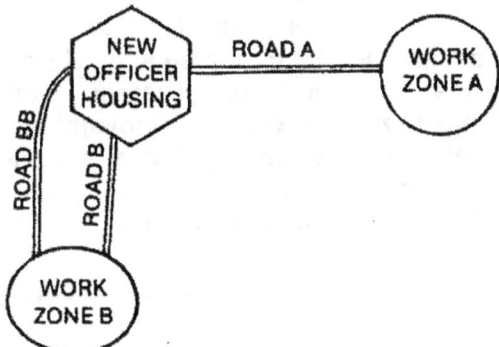

200 TRIPS

300 TRIPS

④ TRIP ASSIGNMENT*
Over which routes will trips between activities be made?

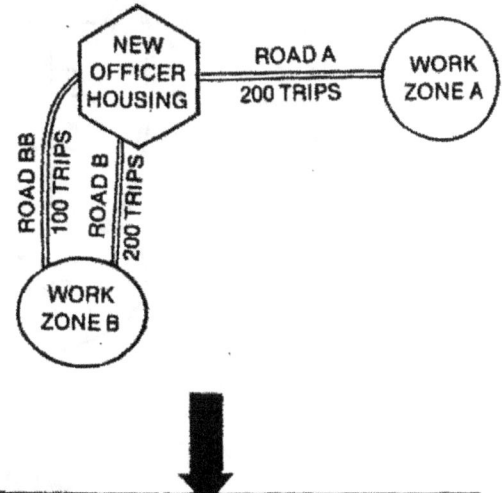

ROAD A 200 TRIPS

100 TRIPS

200 TRIPS

*Only peak-hour trips in direction of maximum flow are shown.

TRAVEL PROJECTIONS

① LAND USE — Where will activities be located?

LAND-USE FORECASTS *provide estimates of future land development — location and type. These estimates* include not only *land usage,* but also *socio-economic variables, such as population, dwelling units, retail sales.* On military installations, this information is obtained from the installation master development plan. However, a major consideration in selecting locations shown on the development plan is the accessibility of that location. Therefore, as the road system is developed, proposed land uses shown on the development plan should be reexamined and changed, if necessary, to achieve a desirable future travel pattern. In every case, the road plan should provide a circulation system that maximizes access for movements between activities, giving due consideration to safety, comfort, and convenience, as well as cost.

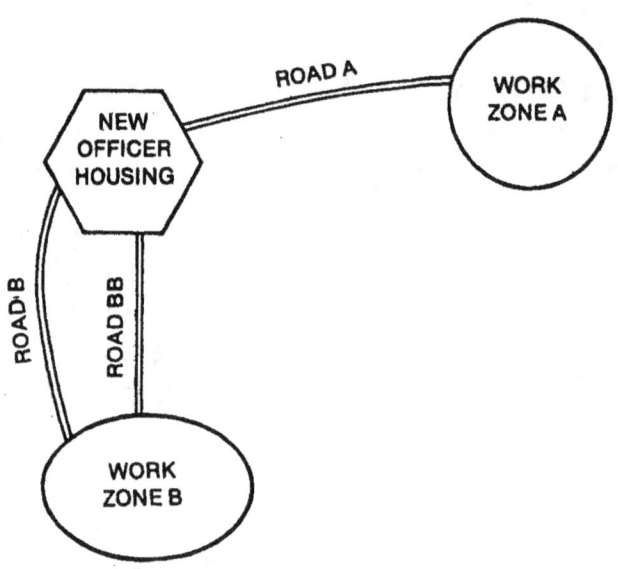

PREDICTIONS OF FUTURE TRAVEL ARE BASED ON FUTURE LAND USE

AND USE PLANNING OBJECTIVES

- Plan for people — not for automobiles and buildings.
- Arrange facilities to achieve the most attractive working and living environment.
- Improve internal traffic flow and external access.
- Consolidate various functional activities.
- Lay out commercial facilities in a way that will bring the patrons close to as many stores as possible once they have parked.
- Locate industrial sites adjacent to transportation facilities so that access is as convenient as possible.
- Provide space for future expansion of facilities and for offstreet parking.
- Locate pollution- and noise-emitting facilities away from residential and commercial areas.
- Route as much traffic as possible around dwelling areas.
- Separate pedestrian and vehicle flows.
- Provide locations that are convenient to residential areas for supplemental services — parks, schools, shops, and chapels.

② TRIP GENERATION — How many trips begin or end at an activity?

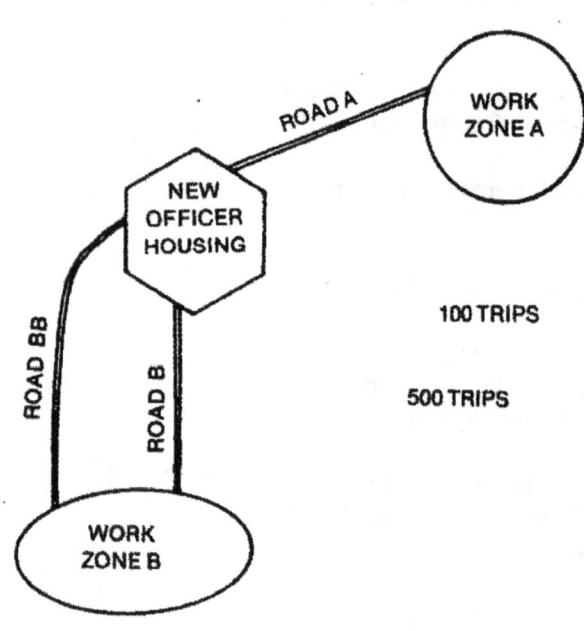

TRIP GENERATION DETERMINES PARKING AND ACCESS NEEDS

TRIP GENERATION ANALYSIS is a way to *estimate the number of future trips that will begin or end at an activity.* Trip generation analysis provides information on the peak volume of cars to be parked and the peak volume of traffic to be moved onto the road system at any one time.

Trip generation predictions are usually based on trip-making rates that are observed at existing facilities. Because of the many variables affecting traffic generation, specific generation rates have not been developed in this guide. However, for most military installations, trip-making rates can be determined from simple counts of vehicles entering and leaving driveways at existing similar facilities. When establishing generation rates, three characteristics of land use should be evaluated: intensity, character, and location of activity. "Intensity of land use" helps relate how many people will use the land and is expressed in such terms as "employees," "1,000 square feet of floor space," and "dwelling units." "Character of land use" refers to the type of land use, such as residential or industrial; whereas, "location of activity" generally refers to either a central built-up area or a remote area. When using existing facilities to estimate trip generation rates, both facilities should be similar in intensity, character, and location.

TYPICAL GENERATION UNITS

LAND USE	UNIT	LAND USE	UNIT
Bank	1,000 sq ft GFA*	Industrial	employee
Bank, drive-in	drive-in window	Institutional (schools)	student & employee
Barracks	person	Library	1,000 sq ft GFA*
Bowling alley	1,000 sq ft GFA*	Military installation	employee
Cafeteria	seat	Office building	employee
Chapel	seat	Recreation facilities	military strength
Clubs	member	Research facility	employee
Commercial	1,000 sq ft GFA*	Restaurant	seat
Dental clinic	dental chair	Service station	pump
Family housing	dwelling unit	Theater	seat
Golf club	member	Visitor center	employee
Guest house	bedroom	Warehouse	employee
Hospital	outpatient & employee		

*Gross floor area

EXAMPLE GENERATION

A. **STATE PROBLEM AND NEED**

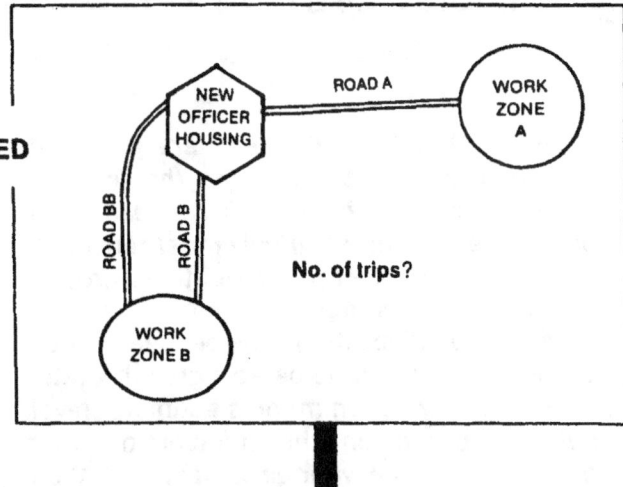

B. **IDENTIFY LAND-USE FACTORS**
- LOCATION
- CHARACTER
- INTENSITY

- BUILT-UP AREA
- RESIDENTIAL
- 500 HOUSES

C. **DEVELOP GENERATION RATE**
(Relation between trip making and land use at similar facility)

SURVEY AT SIMILAR FACILITY
- BUILT-UP AREA
- 400 HOUSES
- RESIDENTIAL
- 400 CARS EXITING IN PEAK HOUR
- TRIP RATE = 1.0 TRIPS/HOUSE

D. **APPLY RELATIONSHIP TO FORECAST**

- PEAK-HOUR ACCESS DEMAND = (500 HOUSES) (1.0 TRIPS/HOUSE)
  = 500 TRIPS

* Only peak-hour trips in direction of maximum flow are shown.

③ TRIP DISTRIBUTION — How many trips will be made between activities?

TRIP DISTRIBUTIONS *are analyzed to establish the number of trips that will be made between specific activity areas.* Two basic types of *mathematical models* are used to predict future trip distribution: *growth models* and *distribution models.* Growth models expand existing trips between zones based on an anticipated growth rate; whereas, *distribution models* estimate travel patterns based on the number of trips generated by the various zones, and then distribute these trips among the zones. The better known traffic models include the Fratar, Gravity, Intervening Opportunities, and Competing Opportunities. However, since these models require sophisticated data collection and analyses, they are not generally used at relatively small military installations.

TRIP DISTRIBUTION AT A MILITARY INSTALLATION generally can be *accomplished through* two methods. *An average-growth factor method* is used where significant changes in the zonal characteristics are not expected. When areas are almost completely undeveloped, a *proportional distribution method* is used. Both methods present reasonably accurate predictions of the future home-to-work trip. The average-growth method projects future trips between two zones by applying an average of the two zonal growth rates to the existing trips between the zones. On the other hand, the distribution method simply proportions the trips to be generated at a new facility in relation to existing concentrations at trip origins. Relationships for use in these models can be developed from origin and destination studies and/or peak-hour traffic counts.

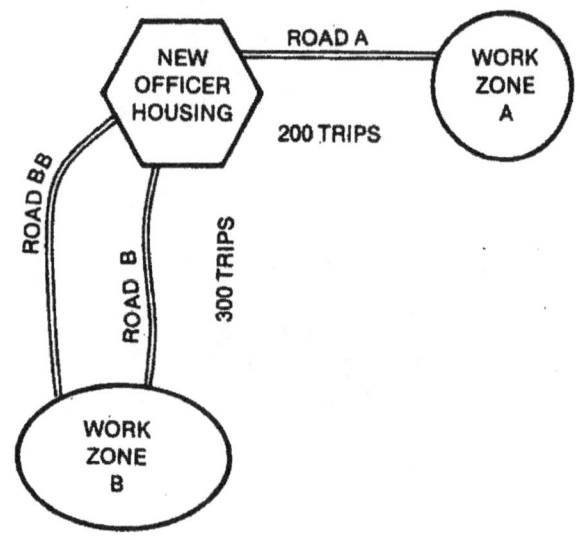

TRIP DISTRIBUTION DETERMINES TRAFFIC CORRIDOR

EXAMPLE DISTRIBUTION*

I. GROWTH MODEL

Where:

$$T_{ij} = t_{ij}\left(\frac{F_i + F_j}{2}\right)$$

T_{ij} = future trips between i & j
t_{ij} = existing trips between i & j
F_i = growth factor at i
F_j = growth factor at j

Ⓐ DETERMINE NUMBER OF EXISTING TRIPS BETWEEN ZONES

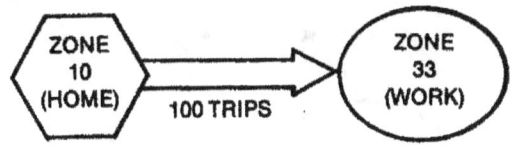

(FROM ORIGIN AND DESTINATION SURVEYS)

Ⓑ ESTIMATE GROWTH RATES FOR BOTH ZONES

$$F_{10} = 1.6$$
$$F_{33} = 1.4$$

(INSTALLATION GROWTH ESTIMATES FROM MASTER DEVELOPMENT PLAN)

Ⓒ COMPUTE FUTURE TRIPS

$$T_{10,33} = t_{10,33}\left(\frac{F_{10} + F_{33}}{2}\right)$$
$$= 100\left(\frac{1.6 + 1.4}{2}\right)$$
$$= 150 \text{ TRIPS}$$

II. DISTRIBUTION MODEL

Where:

$$T_{ij} = T_j\left(\frac{P_i}{\sum_{i=1}^{n} P_i}\right)$$

T_{ij} = future trips between i and j
T_j = future trips generated at j
P_i = existing trips produced at i
$\sum_{i=1}^{n} P_i$ = total trips produced

Ⓐ DETERMINE TRIPS TO BE GENERATED AT NEW FACILITY

500 HOUSING UNITS WILL GENERATE 500 TRIPS

Ⓑ FROM TRAVEL SURVEYS DETERMINE WHERE EXISTING TRIPS ARE DISTRIBUTED

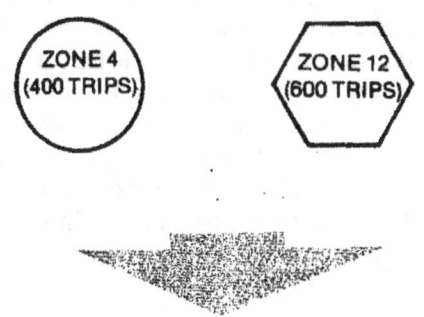

Ⓒ DISTRIBUTE FUTURE TRIPS PROPORTIONATELY

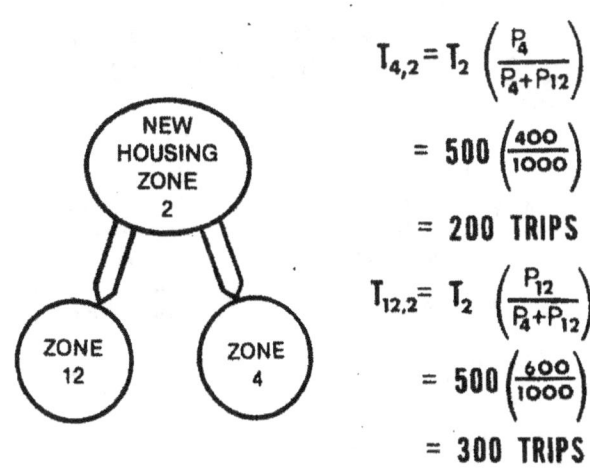

$$T_{4,2} = T_2\left(\frac{P_4}{P_4 + P_{12}}\right)$$
$$= 500\left(\frac{400}{1000}\right)$$
$$= 200 \text{ TRIPS}$$

$$T_{12,2} = T_2\left(\frac{P_{12}}{P_4 + P_{12}}\right)$$
$$= 500\left(\frac{600}{1000}\right)$$
$$= 300 \text{ TRIPS}$$

*Only peak-hour trips in direction of maximum flow are shown.

④ TRIP ASSIGNMENT — Over which routes will trips between activities be made?

The final phase of forecasting the travel demand is THE ASSIGNMENT OF VEHICLE TRIPS BETWEEN ZONES TO VARIOUS TRAFFIC ROUTES. One method of trip assignment is to simulate, from input on the travel pattern or desires of motorists, the extent to which a proposed system would be used. This technique is very complex; therefore, its use should be limited to those familiar with it.

On a military installation, the *primary technique for assigning traffic* is the *"all or nothing with capacity restraint."* In this technique, trips are allocated between zones to the one single path or route that represents the best path for a certain number of vehicles. Assignment thereafter is made to the second or next best alternate route. Frequently, the maximum traffic on a roadway is established as that capacity at which traffic can flow with only limited congestion, allowing the motorist to travel at his desired pace within legal limits. To achieve a balance in all zone-to-zone traffic, a trial-and-error assignment method generally is used; that is, minimum paths are calculated, assignments are made, roads are analyzed for travel comfort and convenience, then new assignments are made. This process continues until traffic is balanced on all routes between zones.

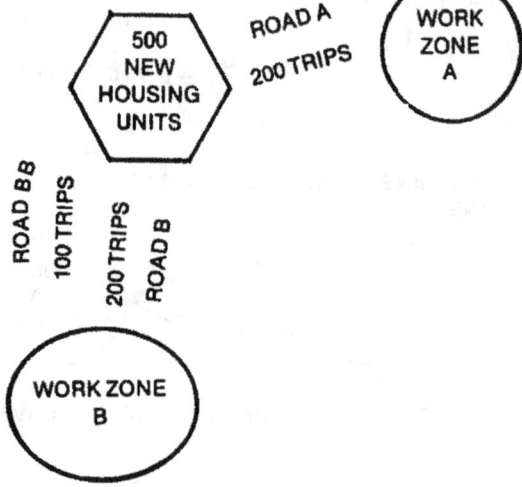

TRIP ASSIGNMENT DETERMINES ROAD WIDTH

FACTORS INFLUENCING ROUTE SELECTION

TANGIBLE	INTANGIBLE
Travel time	Human nature
Travel distance	Relative comfort and ease
Operating cost	Esthetics
Frequency of stops	Geometrics
Safety	

COMPONENTS OF ASSIGNED TRAFFIC

INDUCED TRAFFIC — new trips enticed

DIVERTED TRAFFIC — existing trips diverted from other paths

FACILITY-CREATED TRAFFIC — sightseers o[r] traffic developed because of changes in land use

CONVERTED TRAFFIC — change in mode, such as bus to auto or auto-pool to driver

SHIFTED TRAFFIC — existing trips that show new origin and/or destination

NATURAL GROWTH TRAFFIC — result of natural growth rate

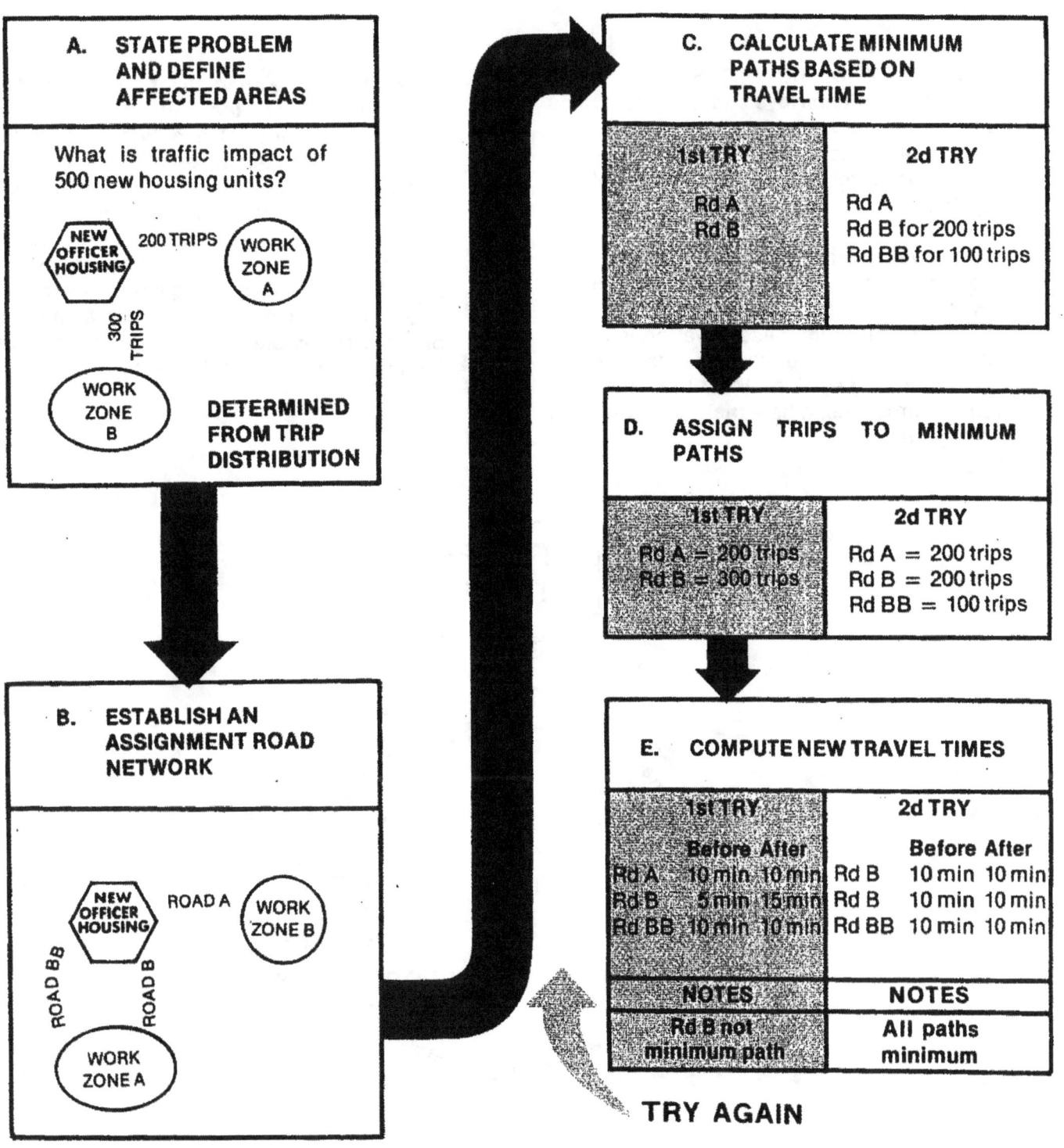

*Only peak-hour trips in direction of maximum flow are shown.

THIS PHASE OF ROAD DESIGN concerns **reducing traffic surveys and travel forecasts into various acceptable road systems.** The goal statements discussed in chapter 2 provide a basis for determining an acceptable system.

The development of alternatives, which by nature is a creative function, usually begins by estimating future travel on the existing road system. From these travel projections, problem areas and road needs can be identified. Assuming that this measure shows problems, a new trial road system is designed.

Once **one or more alternatives** are developed, the road plans are then tested to examine their performance. Congestion should be tested first. As alternatives pass the congestion test, they should be measured in more detail, such as travel time, travel distance, safety, parking, user costs, and environmental impact. The development and testing should end with a manageable number of alternatives that are acceptable in all phases of the roadway plan test. These alternatives then pass into the selection stage.

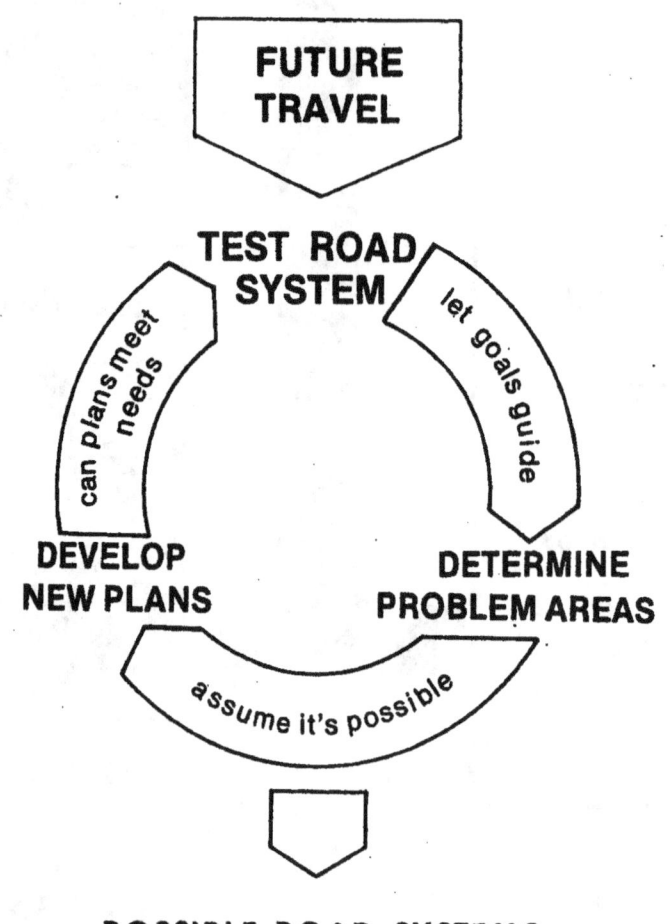

Although development is a creative function, the following objectives should be used to enhance the creative capacity of the road designer.

1 REDUCE CONGESTION

The test of any road system starts by measuring its capacity to handle projected traffic volumes. To eliminate capacity problems, the planner should not only insure that the congested roadways are improved, but should also consider improving remote routes in the vicinity, or even adding entire segments. For example, a bypass road can help relieve congestion on routes that are remote from it.

2 SERVE TRIP DESIRES

Analysis of vehicle trips — their origin, destination, length, and other characteristics — helps to determine installation roadway network, access-road needs, and entrance gate locations.

3 PROVIDE LAND-USE ACCESS

Alternate road systems should be developed to serve access needs identified by the installation master development plan.

4 PROVIDE SYSTEM CONTINUITY

Geometric configurations of the alternate road system should be limited to provide travel continuity, as well as practical construction and operation. When new routes are constructed, they should connect to the existing system where sufficient capacity exists to absorb the additional demand.

DEVELOPMENT OBJECTIVES

1. Reduce congestion
2. Serve trip desires
3. Provide land-use access
4. Provide system continuity

EVALUATION

IN THE EVALUATION, *all acceptable alternatives are considered and compared with one another to determine the best roadway plan.* The plan selected should provide the installation with a traffic corridor system that shows a road type or improvement for each traffic corridor. At this stage, the road plan does not show exact road location. However, each plan presented for evaluation has been found acceptable in the development phase, based on a preliminary look at the possibilities for location and design. In the evaluation phase, one plan is selected; then, in the implementation phase, the final plan is refined to show roadway location and design.

The most common method of evaluating a roadway is simply **to examine the measures of each alternative and make a judgment-based decision.** This decision usually requires trade-offs. For example, "X" minutes saved in travel are worth "Y" dwelling unit removals. As an aid in evaluating trade-offs, a weighting system applied to each evaluation criterion is suggested.

ALTERNATIVE A		ALTERNATIVE B
	EVALUATION	
	BEST PLAN ALTERNATIVE A	

EVALUATION DETERMINES BEST PLAN

EVALUATION METHOD

① ESTABLISH CRITERIA

- Accident rates
- Travel time
- Travel distance
- Exposure to pollution

② DETERMINE WEIGHT OF EACH CRITERION

CRITERIA	WEIGHT
Accident rate	4
Travel time	3
Exposure to pollution	2
Travel distance	1

③ SPECIFY RELATIVE PERFORMANCE OF EACH ALTERNATIVE IN EACH CATEGORY

CRITERIA	PERFORMANCE RATING	
	ALT A	ALT B
Accident rate	2	1
Travel time	2	1
Exposure to pollution	1	2
Travel distance	1	2

④ MULTIPLY THE WEIGHT OF EACH CRITERION BY THE PERFORMANCE RATING, THEN SUM PRODUCTS

CRITERIA	ALT A WEIGHT × PERFORMANCE RATING = PRODUCT	ALT B WEIGHT × PERFORMANCE RATING = PRODUCT
Accident rate	4 × 2 = 8	4 × 1 = 4
Travel time	3 × 2 = 6	3 × 1 = 3
Exposure to pollution	2 × 1 = 2	2 × 2 = 4
Travel distance	1 × 1 = 1	1 × 2 = 2
Total	17	13

⑤ SELECT BEST PLAN

ALT A

IMPLEMENTATION

ROADWAY IMPLEMENTATION includes location, design, right-of-way acquisition, and construction. It is not a part of the roadway planning process. Planning is only a tool for making decisions today that will meet the roadway needs of tomorrow. However, continual planning provides data and assistance for the implementation. For example, a major service is the supply of base data for locating and designing the roadway within the traffic corridor.

SURVEILLANCE AND REAPPRAISAL

ONE CHARACTERISTIC OF TRANSPORTATION PLANS is that the analysis of a few years ago may be almost obsolete today. Obsolescence of the transportation plan may be caused by changes in goals, shifts of emphasis among goals, changes in funding, changes in administration, and improvements in transportation planning. Obsolescence of the plan is also frequently caused by radical departure from some part of the plan. Each installation should monitor changes that affect the transportation plan and should estimate their effect on the validity of the plan, changing the plan as necessary.

TRAFFIC ENGINEERING

ROAD DESIGN: CATEGORIES OF STREETS

CONTENTS

	Page
I. ARTERIALS	1
ACCESS CONTROL	2
ELEMENTS	6
STAGE DEVELOPMENT	8
II. COLLECTOR AND LOCAL STREETS	9
COLLECTOR	10
LOCAL	11
III. RESIDENTIAL STREETS	12
CLASSIFICATION	13
LAYOUT	14
ELEMENTS	17

ROAD DESIGN: CATEGORIES OF STREETS

I. ARTERIALS

ACCESS CONTROL

ELEMENTS

STAGE DEVELOPMENT

ARTERIALS *are those streets that provide high-volume traffic service.* In the development of an installation road network, the routes selected for arterials usually include portions of existing street systems originally designed to provide land access. This access function conflicts directly with that of providing high-volume traffic service; that is, **for arterial streets, unlimited access equates to poor traffic service in terms of travel time and safety.** This chapter discusses techniques for controlling access to existing arterial streets and provides guidelines for designing new arterials.

ARTERIALS PROVIDE HIGH LEVEL TRAFFIC SERVICE

ACCESS CONTROL

"ACCESS CONTROL" refers to *techniques for reducing traffic interference from intersections and driveways;* it can **vary from full control to none at all.** *Full control is provided with frontage roads and grade separations; partial control, with curb-cut restrictions.* No control permits unlimited access from intersections and driveways. Since most installation arterials must provide some form of land access, this section prescribes ways to provide quality access as related primarily to safety. Quality access can be achieved by improving whole roadway sections or individual intersections and driveway connections.

This chapter describes the techniques for controlling access along roadway sections that have closely spaced driveway connections.

ACCESS CONTROL REDUCES TRAFFIC INTERFERENCE

INSTALL TWO-WAY, LEFT-TURN LANE

This technique *removes left-turning vehicles from the through traffic lanes.* Its major design requirement is a center lane that is at least 14 feet wide. The technique is warranted on multilane roads that meet all of the following criteria: the roadway connects with closely spaced driveways that have per-mile left-turn maneuvers totaling 20 percent of through volume during peak travel periods; the road volume exceeds 10,000 vehicles per day and the road speed exceeds 30 miles per hour. Locations with high accident rates resulting from left-turn maneuvers, will warrant this technique even if they do not meet the criteria required above. A 35-percent reduction in the accident rate can be expected where this technique is used.

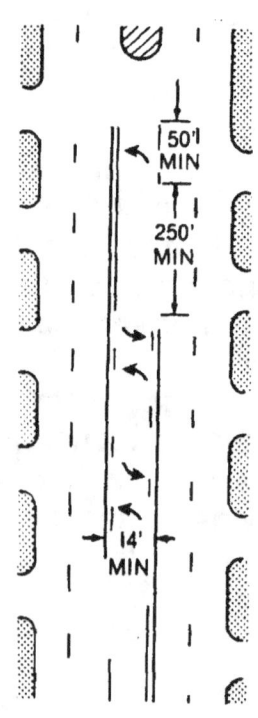

INSTALL RAISED MEDIAN DIVIDER WITH LEFT-TURN DECELERATION LANES

This median treatment *controls access by permitting left turns at major driveways only.* This tight control should yield a 50-percent reduction in total accidents. The price for such safety, however, is the increased travel time and the inconvenience resulting from circuitous travel paths, plus the expense of widening the existing roadway to accommodate median construction. The minimum roadway width for this technique, to accommodate four 11-foot through lanes and a 12-foot median, is 56 feet. A more desirable design requires a road width of 70 feet, with four 12-foot through lanes and a 22-foot median. This technique generally is warranted at locations where the ADT exceeds 10,000 vehicles per day, the travel speed ranges from 30 to 45 miles per hour, and left-turn movements exceed 150 vehicles per hour per mile during the peak period; or where warranted by a high accident rate.

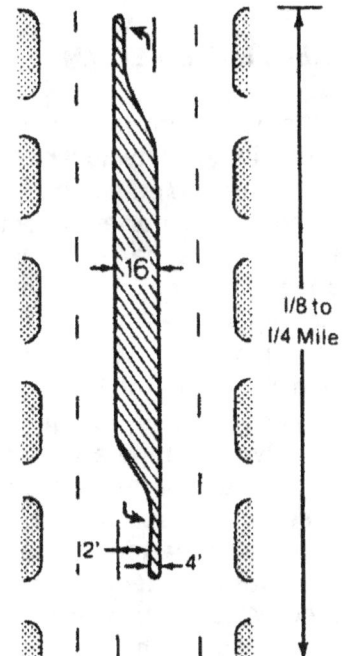

INSTALL ALTERNATING LEFT-TURN LANE

This technique *provides a separate left-turn lane for one direction of traffic at a time into closely spaced driveways.* It has the advantage of requiring a center lane only 12 feet wide, versus the usual 14 feet. This lane design normally can be provided on arterial sections where the traffic volume and travel speeds exceed 10,000 vehicles per day and 30 miles per hour, respectively, and where left turns per mile exceed 15 percent of through traffic during peak traffic demand, or where warranted by accident rates resulting from left-turn maneuvers. In either case, this technique will be used only when other left-turn techniques are infeasible. This technique should produce a 25-percent reduction in the accident rate.

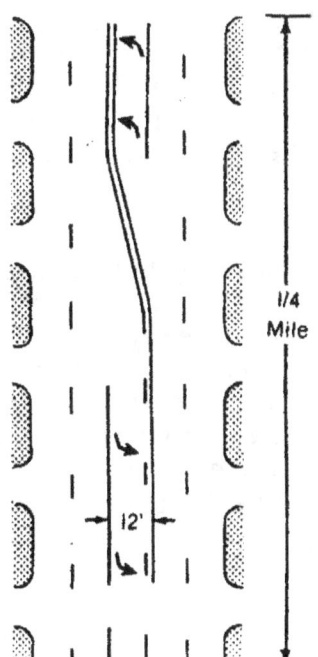

CHANNELIZE THE MEDIAN

This technique controls driveway access by providing a physical barrier to prevent left turns. Median channelization is warranted on arterial sections with 30 driveways per mile, with a travel speed between 30 and 45 miles per hour, and with an ADT of at least 5,000 vehicles per day, but with no more than 100 prohibited left turns per day. In particular, it is warranted where safety is hampered by a few left-turn maneuvers. As this technique causes circuitous routings, the total circulation pattern should be analyzed before the technique is implemented. When it has been determined that median channelization is appropriate for an arterial roadway, the technique can be implemented by three methods.

The first method extends the median to physically prevent left turns from a driveway onto the arterial. This method, common on divided roads with left-turn deceleration lanes at major driveways, should reduce accident rates by 20 percent. For this design, the median must be at least 14 feet wide.

The second method channelizes the median to prevent left turns from the arterial into driveways; but permits left turns from driveways onto the arterial. This method, generally associated with an existing opening in a narrow median, is estimated to reduce accident rates by 30 percent.

The third method closes the median, thus preventing all left turns. This method, common for narrow medians, can be expected to reduce the accident rate by 50 percent.

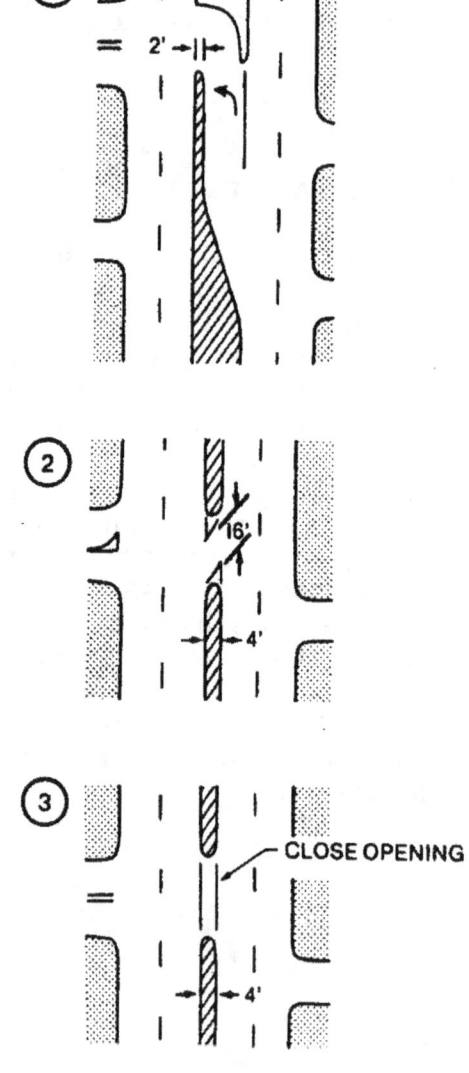

INSTALL CONTINUOUS RIGHT-TURN LANE

A continuous right-turn lane removes turning vehicles from the through traffic stream, thereby reducing the frequency and severity of rear-end collisions. The design is essentially a right-turn lane extended to accommodate several nearby driveways. However, to operate as intended, the continuous lane should be no longer than one-quarter mile; it should be limited to arterial sections with more than 60 driveways per mile, with an ADT exceeding 15,000 vehicles per day, with a travel speed exceeding 30 miles per hour, and with right turns per mile exceeding 20 percent of the ADT.

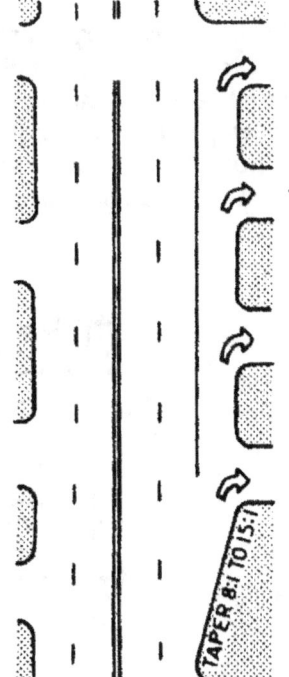

INSTALL ONE-WAY TRAFFIC FLOW

The implementation of one-way operation on arterial sections is an alternate to the previously described medial-design techniques and should be considered where insufficient right-of-way exists for widening the arterial. This technique, which eliminates opposing left-turn conflicts, can *increase capacity* by as much as *50 percent* and improve safety significantly. A *25-percent reduction in total accidents* may be expected after converting to one-way operations.

One-way operations can be initiated usually by converting all traffic lanes to one direction of travel. Of course, use of this technique depends on the availability of a suitable arterial to carry reverse-direction traffic. A pair of closely spaced, one-way streets is suggested.

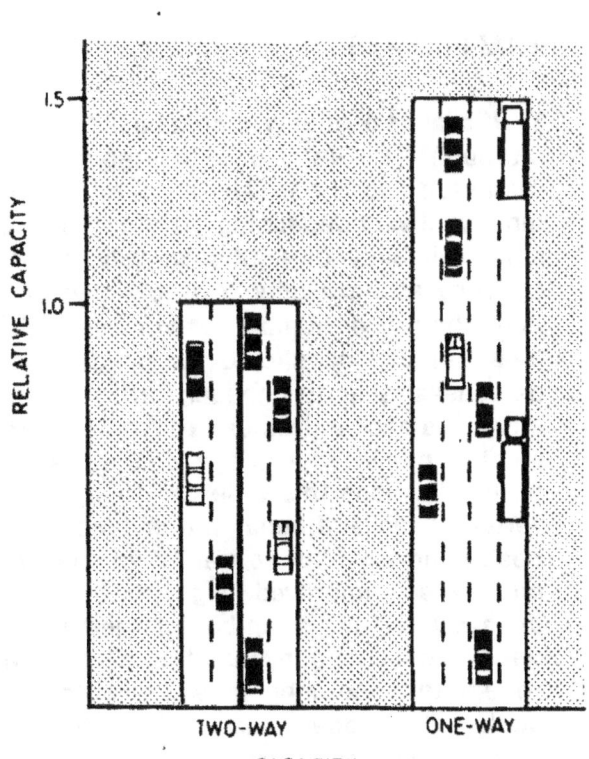

6

ELEMENTS

ARTERIALS usually **carry a large percentage of the total traffic**, with traffic volumes ranging from 8,000 to more than 20,000 vehicles per day; therefore, their **geometric design** should afford high capacity and relatively high speeds. The travel speed along arterials should average between 25 and 35 miles per hour during peak traffic. Therefore, design speeds should range from 40 to 60 miles per hour, with an average design speed of 50 miles per hour. A lower design speed may be used in built-up areas or, particularly, for restrictive conditions.

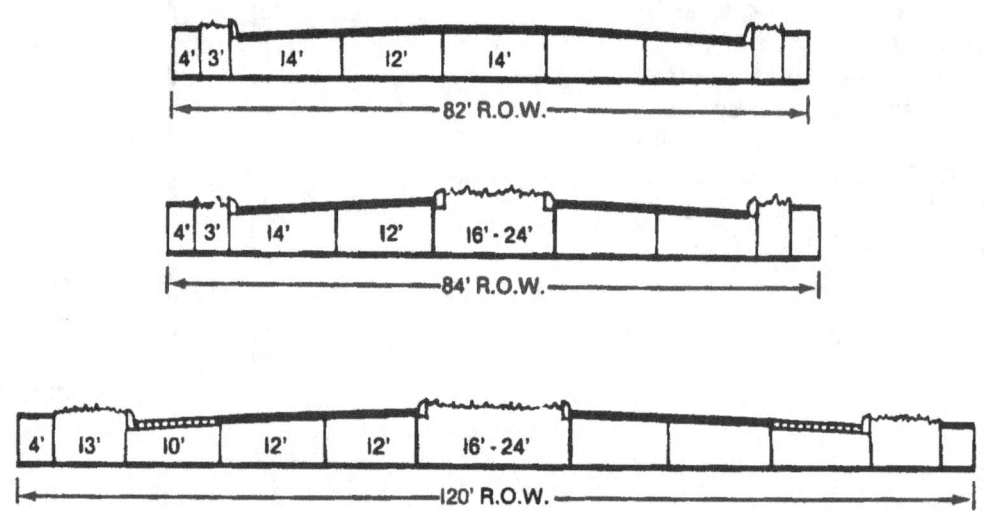

TRAFFIC LANE

Traffic lanes desirably should be 12 feet wide, although 11 feet is acceptable under restricted conditions. The number of traffic lanes will vary depending on traffic demand and availability of right-of-way; however, a capacity analysis should be used to determine the proper number. Use of the road for on-street parking should be avoided, as it decreases capacity, impedes traffic flow, and increases accident potential. Where parking must be permitted, 12-foot-wide lanes should be used. A lane this wide can then be converted to an additional traffic lane during peak hours or if future traffic volumes warrant. Also, improved sight distance at driveway entrances can be obtained without removal of parking, by inserting a no-parking zone, 8 to 10 feet long, between two parking stalls. This added space also facilitates entering and leaving the parking space.

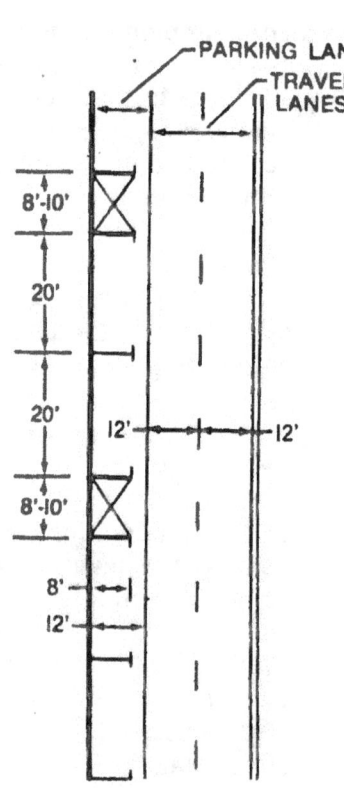

SHOULDERS, CURBS, AND BORDERS

SHOULDERS are an asset to any arterial street. They **enhance safety, serve as speed change lanes for turning vehicles, and provide storage for plowed snow.** On existing arterials, shoulder use may be limited because of restricted right-of-way or the necessity to use available right-of-way for traffic lanes. However, for new roadways with available right-of-way, 10-foot-wide shoulders should be included in the ultimate cross section. Also, every effort should be made to provide borders at least 8, but preferably 12 or more, feet wide. On the other hand, curbs should be omitted unless necessary to control drainage.

SHOULDERS SHOULD BE WIDE ENOUGH TO ACCOMMODATE STOPPED VEHICLE

MEDIANS

MEDIANS, like shoulders, greatly improve the safety of arterials and should be provided as space and funds permit. Limited space and funds add importance in the allocation of space to borders, traffic lanes, and medians. For example, where land access from the roadway is vital, a two-way, left-turn lane may be superior to a raised median. Conversely, where intersections are widely spaced or where lack of space precludes a center lane, the median is preferable, even if it is only a few feet wide. *The most important element of the median is width,* desirably 22 feet to allow U-turns. However, a 16-foot-wide median will provide a 12-foot-wide storage lane and a 4-foot-wide medial separation.

MEDIAN FUNCTION	MINIMUM WIDTH (FT)	DESIRED WIDTH (FT)
Separate opposing traffic	4	10
Pedestrian refuge and sign locations	6	14
Left-turn storage	16	20
U-Turns	22	24
Protection for crossing vehicles	25	30

STAGE DEVELOPMENT

Because of their enormous construction cost, arterial roadways sometimes are developed over a period of years. Also, when new roadways are constructed, traffic volumes may not warrant major-street design. In such cases, stage construction is appropriate. The initial construction can consist of only a 24-foot-wide pavement, offset 8 feet from the center line of a 120-foot- wide right-of-way. At a future date, two lanes can be added to the other side of the center line; also a separate left-turn lane in each direction can be provided from the median at major intersections. The final stage of construction would be the addition of two travel lanes to provide a total of three travel lanes in each direction. Relatively speaking, the ultimate cross-section capacity would be almost five times the initial capacity.

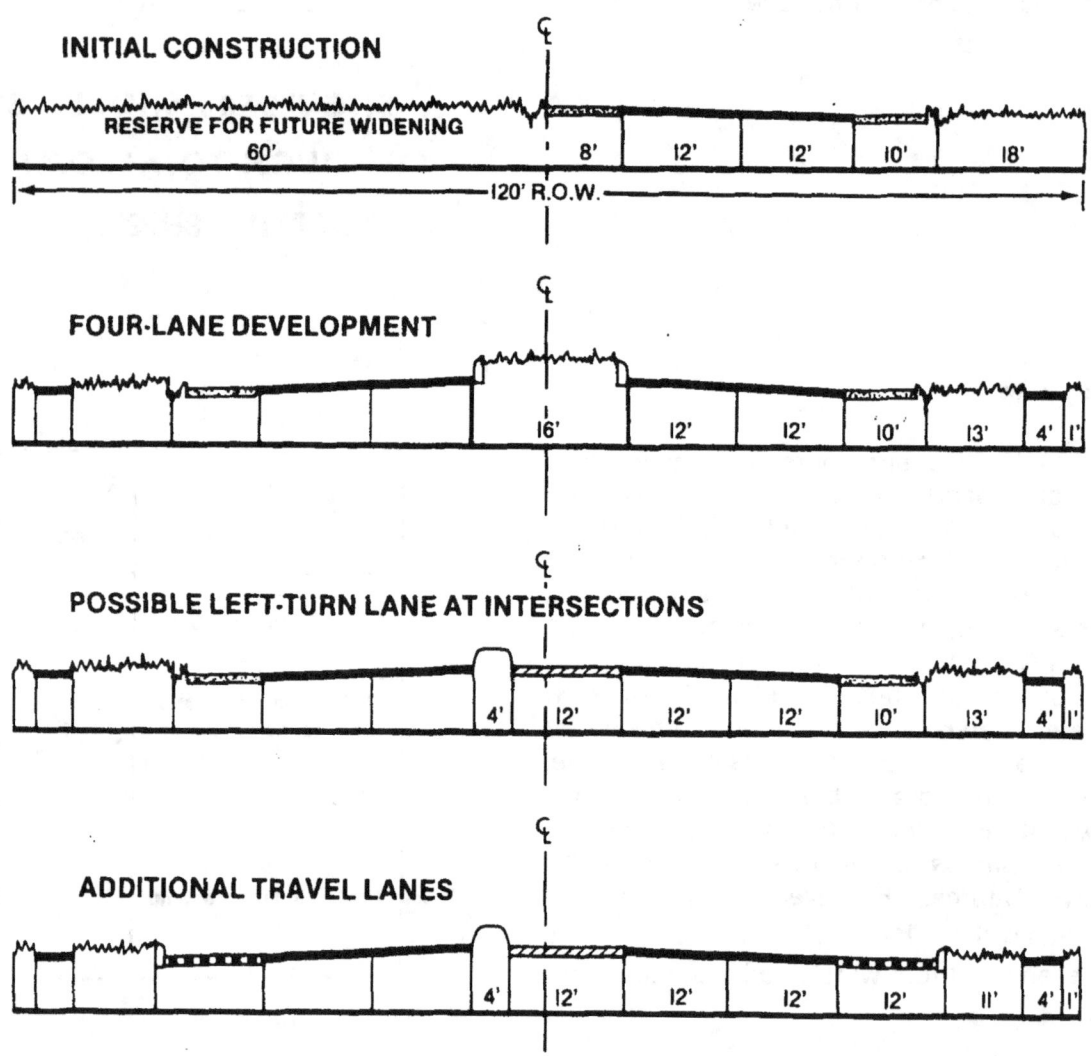

II. COLLECTOR AND LOCAL STREETS

COLLECTOR

LOCAL

Within the classification system for installation roadways, there are **three categories of streets: arterial, collector, and local.** Design of arterial streets, which serve as through streets with limited access, was discussed in chapter I. This chapter discusses design criteria for collector and local streets. **Collector streets** should be designed to serve, about equally, the functions of access to abutting property and through movement; whereas, **local streets** should be designed primarily as access streets for abutting property, and their function as a through street should be minimal.

COLLECTOR AND LOCAL STREETS PROVIDE ACCESS TO ABUTTING PROPERTY

COLLECTOR

Local streets carry limited traffic volume at low speeds; whereas, arterial streets are designed to carry high volumes over greater distances at higher speeds. Design standards for collector streets fall between these two extremes. **Four types of collector streets** are discussed in this guide: **residential, commercial, industrial, and neighborhood.**

RESIDENTIAL

RESIDENTIAL COLLECTORS *are designed to handle traffic volumes of up to 2,000 vehicles per day, while providing access to abutting property and on-street parking.* Such streets are necessary adjacent to multi-family residential developments, schools, and local retail and public facilities. They are required also when more than 50 dwelling units or residential lots must utilize the street for access to the collector/arterial street system. *Major entry streets to a residential community normally will be set up as residential collector streets.* The right-of-way should be 60 feet wide, and the pavement, 44 feet wide.

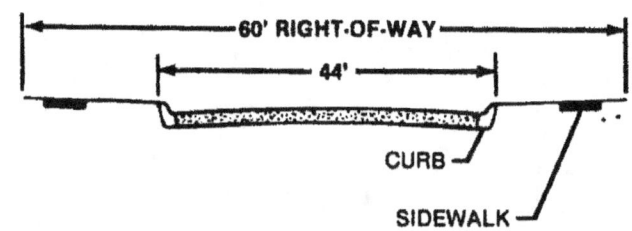

INDUSTRIAL/COMMERCIAL

A COMMERCIAL OR INDUSTRIAL COLLECTOR is one serving as principal access to a commercial development or an industrial site. The length of such a street should not exceed two miles. Direct residential frontage should be discouraged to prevent a conflict between residential and commercial traffic. Multi-family development, BOQ's or BEQ's, can front onto a commercial collector if ample off-street parking is provided and access is limited. For industrial streets, the right-of-way and pavement widths are 80' and 64 feet, respectively; and for commercial streets, 60 and 44 feet, respectively.

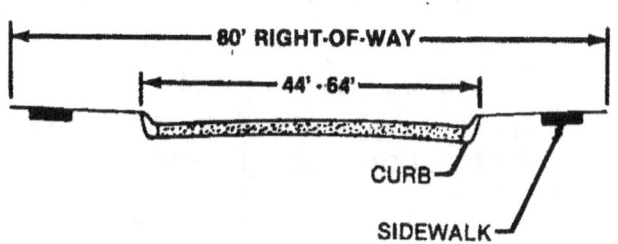

NEIGHBORHOOD

A NEIGHBORHOOD COLLECTOR STREET is designed to traverse distances from one-half to two miles, to serve a variety of land uses, and to handle traffic volumes of up to 8,000 vehicles per day. On-street parking usually is prohibited or restricted on neighborhood collectors; access to abutting property is limited, and uses may include multifamily dwelling units; schools; and retail, office, and community service facilities. Streets in a residential area serving more than 200 dwelling units should be designated as neighborhood collector streets. The right-of-way should be 70 feet wide and the pavement 44 feet wide. At major intersections, left-turn lanes may be required in addition to four through lanes. Where left-turn lanes are required, pavement must be 64 feet wide with an 80-foot-wide right-of-way.

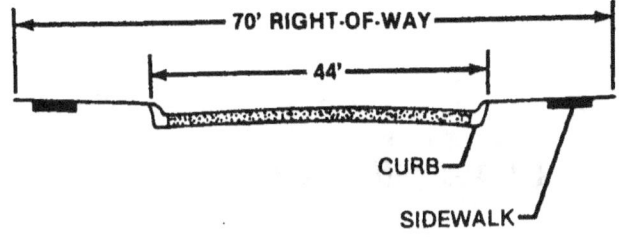

LOCAL STREETS *provide access to abutting property, and parking on these streets is usually permitted.* The main function of these streets is to **link the collector/arterial system and the low-density residential development**, as shown in chapter 10. Also, a few business and industrial streets can be considered in this class. However, due to the potential for increased development along these streets, most commercial streets should be designed as collectors.

Traffic volumes on local streets should be less than 2,000 vehicles per day, and their length less than 3,000 feet. The right-of-way requires a width of 54 feet, and the pavement should have a width of 34 feet.

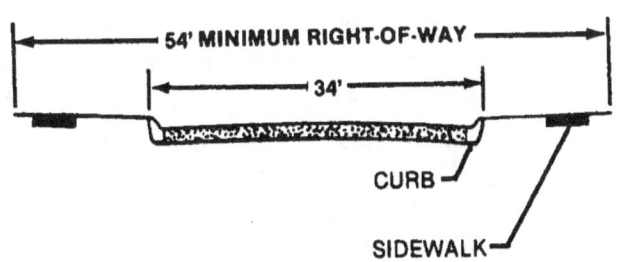

III. RESIDENTIAL STREETS

CLASSIFICATION

LAYOUT

ELEMENTS

RESIDENTIAL LIVING can be enhanced significantly through proper design of the "neighborhood unit," as this *area encompasses most of the major facilities required by its resident population.* Besides the family dwellings themselves, these facilities include elementary schools, churches, shopping centers, recreational facilities, utilities and, not least, streets. This section provides guidance for designing local streets for use in a residential environment.

DESIGN RESIDENTIAL AREAS FOR TODAY'S NEEDS

CLASSIFICATION

Residential streets usually have four classifications: **place, lane, subcollector, or collector.** Each is discussed below.

PLACE

A PLACE is a *short street, cul-de-sac, or court,* whose primary function is to conduct traffic to and from dwelling units to other streets within the neighborhood. Usually, a place is dead-end, with an ADT of less than 100 and with limited on-street parking.

LANE

A LANE is *similar to a place in design and function,* the primary difference being that a lane occasionally branches to connect two or three other lanes or places. Like a place, a lane does not serve through traffic, but its ADT range (75 to 350) is higher than that of a place.

SUBCOLLECTOR

A SUBCOLLECTOR, with an ADT ranging between 200 and 1,000, *provides access to places and lanes and conducts traffic to an activity center or to a street of higher classification.* The subcollector may be a loop connecting one collector or arterial street at two points, or it may be a fairly straight street conducting traffic between collector and/or arterial streets.

COLLECTOR

A COLLECTOR *conducts traffic between arterial streets and/or activity centers.* It is a principal traffic artery within residential areas and carries a relatively high ADT, ranging between 800 and 2,000 vehicles.

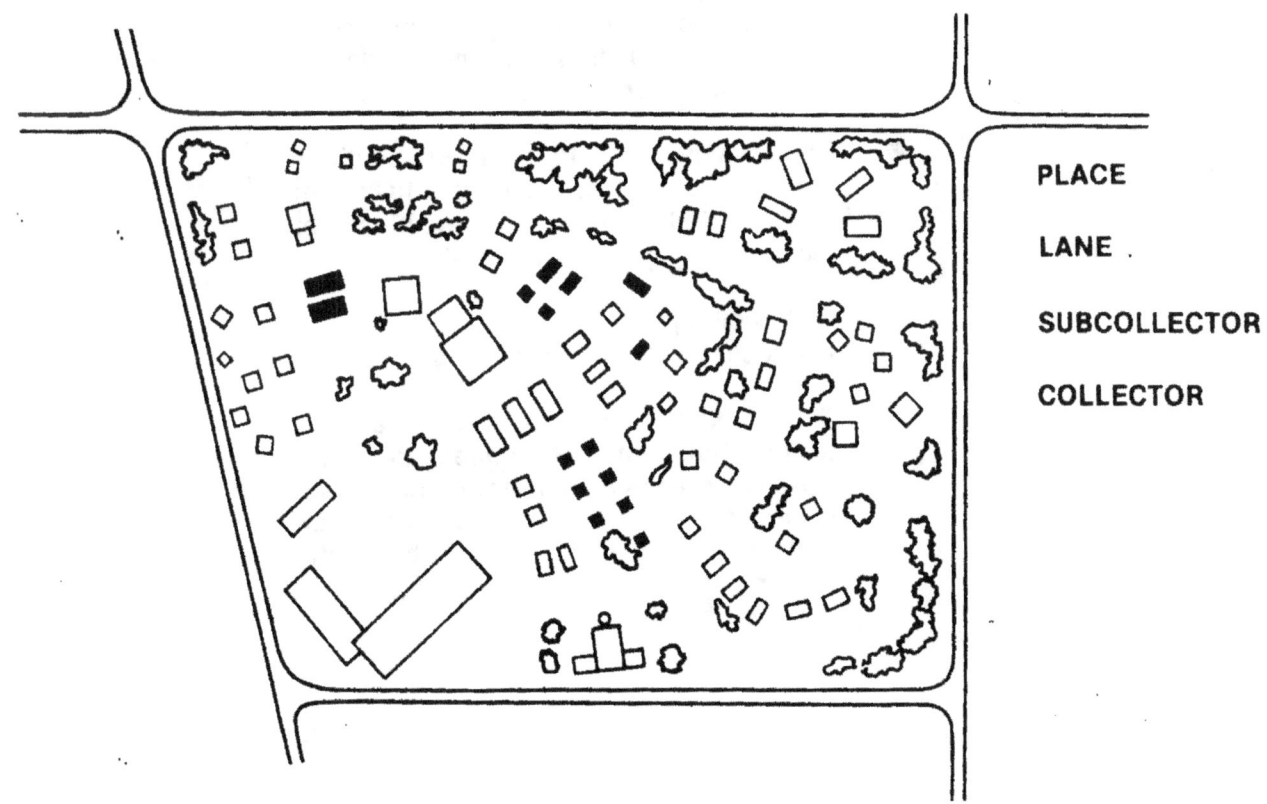

PLACE

LANE

SUBCOLLECTOR

COLLECTOR

LAYOUT

THE BASIC CONCEPT OF A NEIGHBORHOOD is to group land uses away from, but conveniently accessible to, through-traffic arterials.

DESIGN CRITERIA

- The use of through streets, as well as the rectangular grid pattern, should be avoided in the residential network design. Through traffic can be discouraged by creating discontinuities in the street pattern, such as loops and cul-de-sacs.

- Street patterns should be reasonably repetitive or should conform to the topography. Streets that wander or turn back toward themselves should be avoided.

- The specific function of residential streets should be clearly indicated in their design and construction.

- Whenever possible, four-way intersections should be avoided in the residential street layout. Well-spaced T-intersections, at least 150 feet apart, are preferable.

- All dwellings should be accessible to emergency and service vehicles.

- The residential street must be accessible to the traffic it is intended to serve. Driveway grades should not be more than 10 percent; that is, the street should not be more than 5 feet above or 10 feet below the housing unit.

ACCESS CONTROL

TRAFFIC CIRCULATION SYSTEMS AND LAND DEVELOPMENT PATTERNS within the residential area *should not detract from the efficiency of bordering arterial roadways.* Driveway entrances should be avoided on arterial streets and, wherever possible, on collector streets. Intersections along arterials should be placed as shown below for efficient control.

ACCESS DESIGNS

① **REAR LOTTING**  PREFERRED

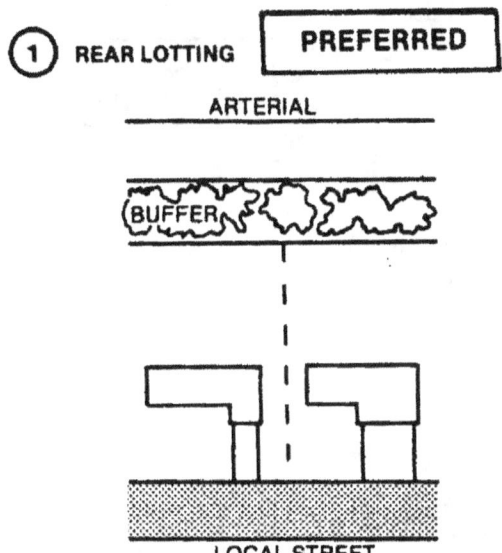

② **ACCESS STREET**

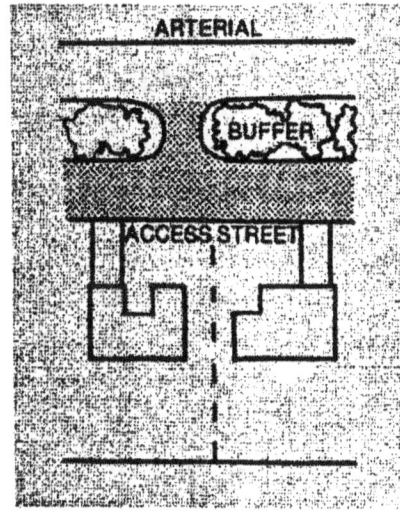

③ **CUL-DE-SAC**

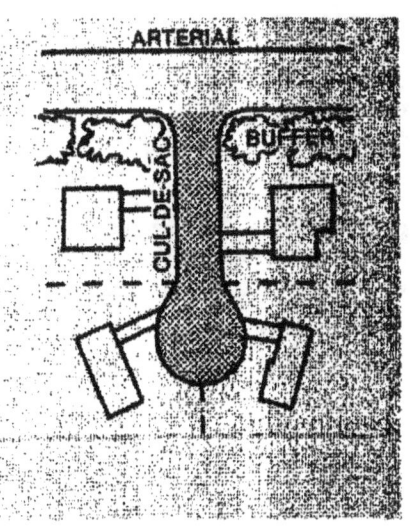

④ **LOOP STREET**

ARRANGEMENT

The arrangement of **LOCAL STREETS** should permit practical patterns, shapes, and lot sizes.

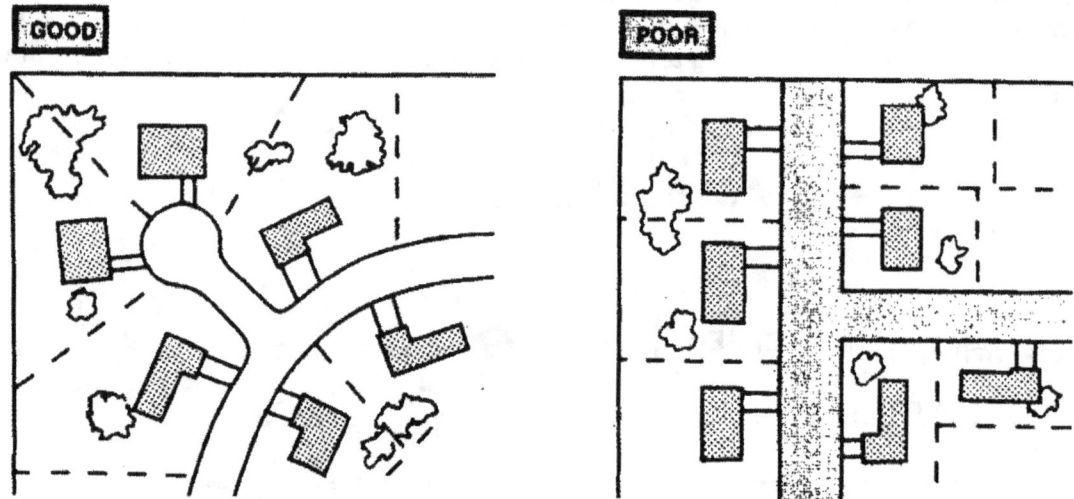

If streets are not to be extended at the corner of the residential area, use curved or cul-de-sac streets.

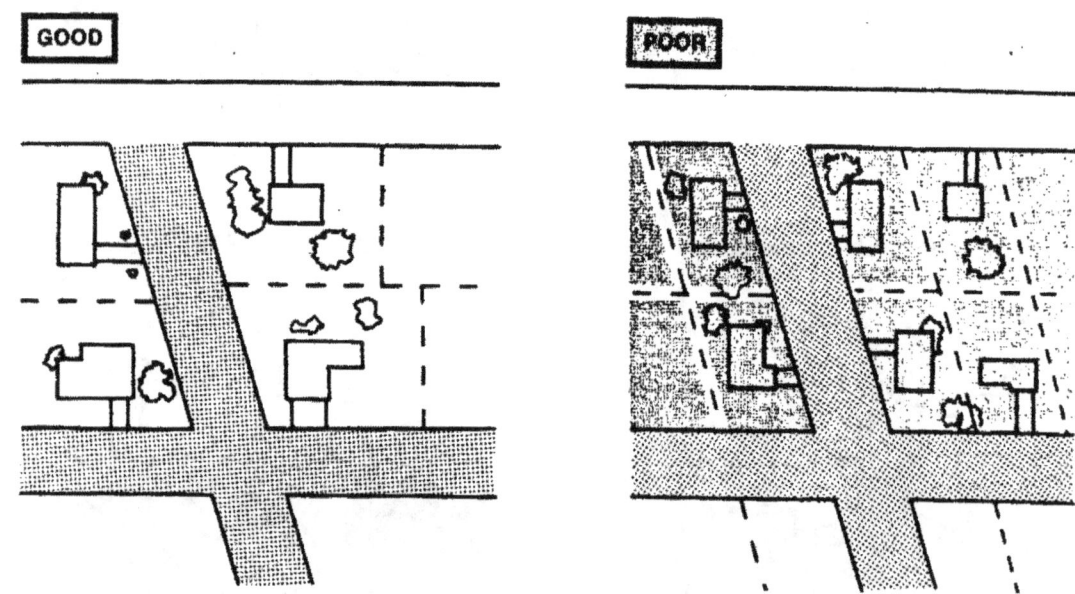

When flat-angled streets must be used, keep lots perpendicular to the major streets.

ELEMENTS

RIGHT-OF-WAY *must be sufficient to contain the elements of pavement and curbing, sidewalks where required, and street utilities.* In extreme northern climates, additional width may be required for snow plowed from the roadway. Allowance for future street widening should be unnecessary in most well-planned neighborhoods. Where future widening is anticipated, right-of-way allowance should be based on the installation master plan.

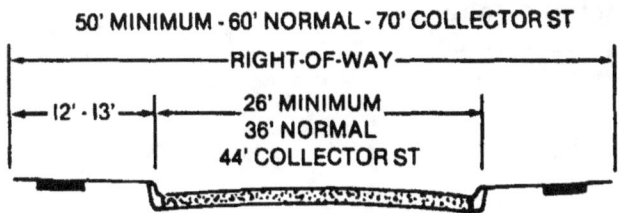

PAVEMENT WIDTH

THE PAVEMENT WIDTH FOR RESIDENTIAL STREETS *varies from 26 to 44 feet.* A 36-foot width, which provides two travel lanes and two on-street parking lanes, is the most common. In restricted areas and low-density housing areas, a 26-foot width is acceptable, as it assures one free-moving traffic lane even when vehicles park on both sides of the street. However, the narrower width should be used only on streets whose travel distance to the nearest collector street is less than 1,500 feet. A pavement width less than 26 feet is not recommended for residential areas. While the pavement is too narrow to permit parking on both sides and still provide one free-moving travel lane, it is wide enough to tempt drivers to park on both sides.

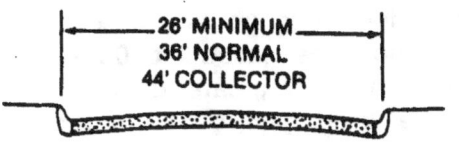

For collector streets, a 44-foot width is recommended, as it will provide two 10-foot-wide parking lanes and two 12-foot-wide travel lanes.

CURBS

CURBS *provide excellent control of drainage, furnish protection for pavement edge, and discourage drivers from encroaching beyond paved surfaces.* For these reasons, curbs are recommended for most residential streets. However, when the sole purpose of the curb is to furnish pavement-edge protection, alternatives to curbs should be considered.

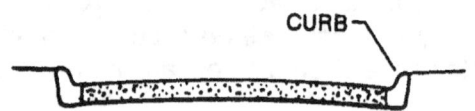

SIDEWALKS

SIDEWALKS along most residential collector streets **are both desirable and necessary.** However, for minor residential streets, sidewalks may not be justified on both sides, or even one side, of the street. In either case, before sidewalks are installed, the expected use of the sidewalk should be evaluated. For example, when residents will include children, and paved private driveways are not planned, sidewalks on at least one side of the street should be installed.

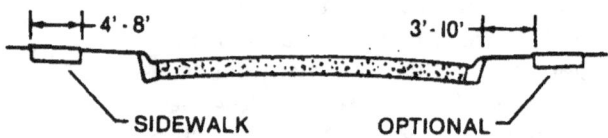

The sidewalk should be at least 4-feet wide, but wider in school areas. Also, the walks should be placed 3 to 10 feet from the curb — the greater distance being preferred along collector streets. In any case, the maximum separation of pedestrians and vehicles is desirable.

PARKING

PARKING for residential areas should be designed so that all residents park off street and only visitor parking overflows onto the street. For low- to medium-density housing areas, at least two off-street spaces should be provided per dwelling unit, and only parallel parking should be permitted on street. For high-density areas, independent studies should be made to determine parking demand and projected needs. Parking bays constructed for these areas should be physically separated from the roadway, using a 90-degree double-bay parking layout.

Another item of increasing importance in residential parking is the recreational vehicle. These vehicles, as well as trailers and other special-purpose vehicles, should not be parked on residential streets, in front yards, or between residences. Ideally, they should be stored and maintained in separate, secured areas provided by the installation.

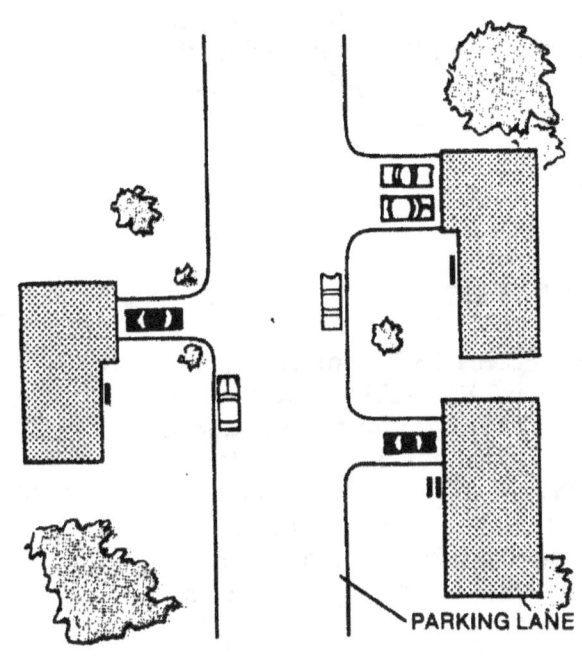

TURNAROUNDS

Modern residential design has led to increased use of CUL-DE-SACS and other DEAD-END roadways. Except on short driveways serving individual dwelling units, every dead-end roadway that might be used by large vehicles should be provided with a turning facility. To accommodate a small truck and a single piece of fire equipment, a 40-foot curb radius is considered minimum. However, where parking is to be provided within the cul-de-sac, a 50-foot radius is recommended.

The usual length of street leading to a turnaround ranges from 400 to 600 feet. When using lengths longer than 500 feet, the maximum number of dwelling units that are provided access should not exceed 20.

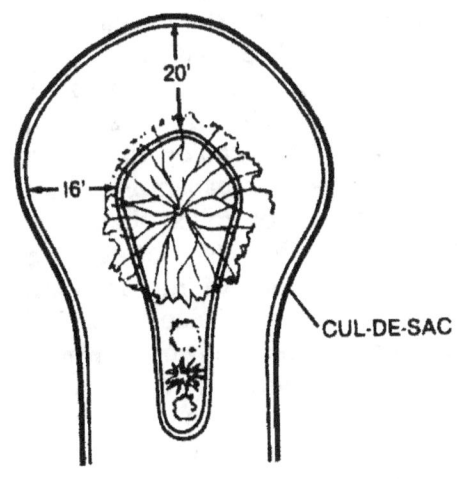

STREET LIGHTING

For safety, security, and convenience, MODERN STREET LIGHTING should be provided at every intersection. Energy savings cannot be justified when the tradeoff involves pedestrian security. To add aesthetic value, underground wiring is recommended.

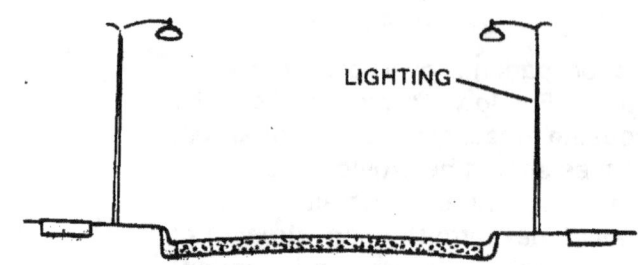

DESIGN SPEED

LOW DESIGN SPEED on residential streets is DESIRABLE. A design speed of 20 to 25 miles per hour is recommended for places and lanes, and 25 to 35 miles per hour for collector streets. The lower speeds of each class should be used for hilly terrain, and the higher speeds for flat and rolling terrain.

SIGHT DISTANCE

A residential roadway network should be designed to operate without any traffic control device, except along collector streets. The need for control devices can best be minimized by maintaining clear sight distance. CLEAR SIGHT DISTANCE, in turn, *can best be provided by properly locating buildings, fences, shrubbery, or trees, and by restricting the height of any embankment.* Sight distance can be controlled also by *intersection location.* When streets are laid out, the placing of intersections on a hilltop or slightly below a hilltop should be avoided. However, where one of these intersections must be used, the hillcrest is preferable because it offers two-directional visibility.

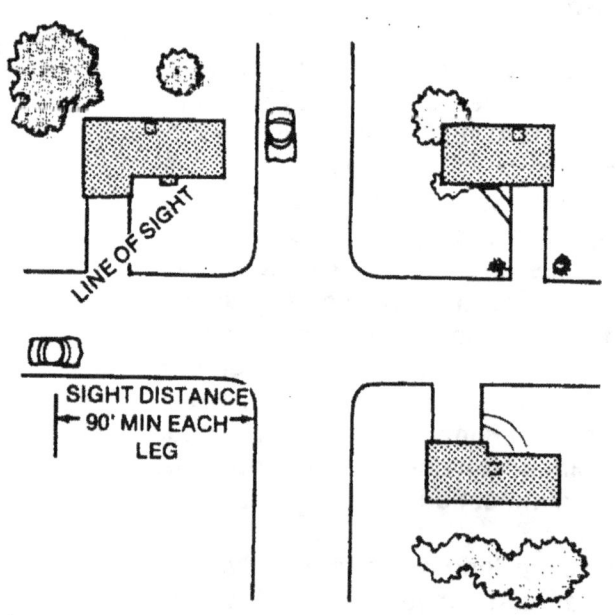

DRAINAGE

Whenever possible, *street layouts should be planned to avoid* EXCESSIVE CONCENTRATION OF STORM RUNOFF. When the residential area is constructed, the structures and the paved roads will increase the stormwater runoff. This runoff should not cross several properties, wash away front yards, or flow from the street to a building site. Therefore, careful curbed-street layout and gradient planning will help route storm runoff to avoid undue concentration on street surfaces or residential property.

STREETS PERPENDICULAR TO CONTOURS

A road that is perpendicular to the contours causes steep yards; as a result, storm runoff accumulates on properties at the bottom of the grade. Retaining walls may be necessary. Special drainage systems are needed to drain water from the lot to the street to prevent house flooding in heavy rains. Roads perpendicular to contours, with grades over 4 or 5 percent, should be avoided.

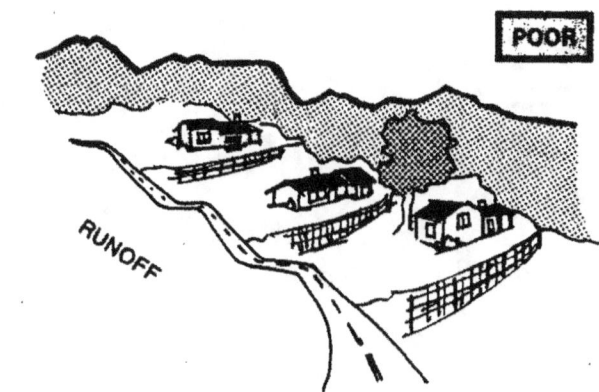

STREET PARALLEL TO CONTOURS

Roads on steep slopes running parallel to the contours will make one house too high to permit driveway connections, while the opposite house will be below street level and will have a poor lot. What's more, it may be impossible to connect the lower house to the sanitary sewer system and achieve gravity flow.

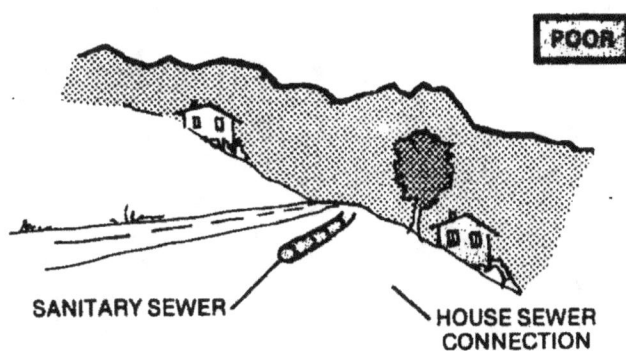

STREET DIAGONAL TO CONTOURS

As explained above, roads over reasonably steep slopes should cut diagonally across contours.

GLOSSARY OF TRAFFIC CONTROL TERMS

TABLE OF CONTENTS

	Page
Access Road ... Desire Line	1
Divided Street ... Left Turn Lane	2
Manual Traffic Control ... Passenger Vehicle	3
Passenger (Transit) Volume ... Separate Turning Lane	4
Shoulder ... Traffic Accident	5
Traffic Actuated Controller ... Uninterrupted Flow	6
Vehicle ... Zone (Origin-Destination Studies)	7

GLOSSARY OF TRAFFIC CONTROL TERMS

A

ACCESS ROAD - Public roads, existing or proposed, needed to provide essential access to military installation and facilities, or to industrial installations and facilities in the activities of which there is specific defense interest. Roads within the boundaries of military reservation are excluded from this definition unless such roads have been dedicated to public use and are not subject to closure.

ACCIDENT SPOT MAP - An area or installation map showing the location of vehicle accidents by means of symbols. Symbols may represent accidents classified as to daylight hours, night hours, injury or death.

ANGLE PARKING - Parking where the longitudinal axes of vehicles form an angle with the alignment of the roadway.

C

CENTER LINE - A line marking the center of a roadway between traffic moving in opposite direction.

COLLISION DIAGRAM - A plan of an intersection or section of roadway on which reported accidents are diagramed by means of arrows showing manner of collision.

COMBINED CONDITION AND COLLISION DIAGRAM - A condition diagram upon which the reported accidents are diagramed by means of arrows showing manner of collision.

CONDITION DIAGRAM - A plan of an intersection or section of roadway showing all objects and physical conditions having a bearing on traffic movement and safety at that location. Usually these are scaled drawings.

CORDON COUNTS - A count of all vehicles and persons entering and leaving a district (cordon area) during a designated period of time.

CORDON AREA - The district bounded by the cordon line and included in a cordon count.

CROSSWALK - Any portion of a roadway at an intersection or elsewhere distinctly indicated for pedestrian crossing by lines or other markings on the surface. Also, that part of a roadway at an intersection included within the connections of the lateral lines of the sidewalks on opposite sides of the traffic way measured from the curbs, or in the absence of curbs, from the edges of the traversable roadway.

D

DELAY - The time consumed while traffic or a specified component of traffic is impeded in its movement by some element over which it has no control usually expressed in seconds per vehicle.

DESIRE LINE - A straight line between the point of origin and point of destination of a trip without regard to routes of travel (used in connection with an origin-destination study).

DIVIDED STREET - A two-way road on which traffic in one direction of travel is separated from that in the opposite direction by a directional separator. Such a road has two or more roadways.

E

85 PERCENTILE SPEED - That speed below which 85 percent of the traffic unit's travel, and above which 15 percent travel.

F

FIXED-TIME CONTROLLER - An automatic controller for supervising the operation of traffic control signals in accordance with a predetermined fixed time cycle and divisions thereof.

FIXED-TIME TRAFFIC SIGNAL - A traffic signal operated by a fixed-time controller.

FLASHING BEACON - A section of a standard traffic signal head, or a similar type device, having a yellow or red lens in each face, which is illuminated by rapid intermittent flashes.

FLASHING TRAFFIC SIGNAL - A traffic control signal used as a flashing beacon.

FLOATING CAR - An automobile driven in the traffic flow at the average speed of the surrounding vehicles.

FLOW DIAGRAM - The graphical representation of the traffic volumes on a road or street network or section thereof, showing by means of bands the relative volumes using each section of roadway during a given period of time, usually 1 hour.

H

HIGH FREQUENCY ACCIDENT LOCATION - A specific location where a large number of traffic accidents have occurred.

I

INTERSECTION APPROACH - That portion of an intersection leg which is used by traffic approaching the intersection.

L

LATERAL CLEARANCE - The distance between the edge of pavement and any lateral obstruction.

LATERAL OBSTRUCTION - Any fixed object located adjacent to the traveled way which reduces the transverse dimensions of the roadway.

LEFT TURN LANE - A lane within the normal surfaced width reserved for left turning vehicles.

M

MANUAL TRAFFIC CONTROL - The use of-hand signals or manually operated devices by traffic control personnel to control traffic.

MANUAL COUNTER - A tallying device which is operated by hand.

MASS TRANSPORTATION - Movement of large groups of persons.

MULTIAXLE TRUCK - A truck which has more than two axles.

O

OCCUPANCY RATIO -The average number-of occupants per vehicle (including the driver).

ODOMETER -A device on a vehicle for measuring the distance traveled, usually as a cumulative total, but sometimes also for individual trips, with an indicator on the instrument panel where it is usually combined with a speedometer indicator, or in the hub of a wheel in some trucks.

OFF-PEAK PERIOD - That portion of the day in which traffic volumes are relatively light.

OFFSET LANES - Additional lanes used for traffic which is heavier in one direction. Also known as unbalanced lanes.

OFF-STREET PARKING - Lots and garages intended for parking entirely off streets and alleys. street and alleys (may be angle or parallel parking) for parking of vehicles.

ORIGIN DESTINATION STUDIES - A study of the origins and destinations of trips of vehicles and passengers. Usually included in the study are all trips within, or passing through, into or out of a selected area.

OVERALL SPEED - The total distance traversed divided by the travel time. Usually expressed in miles per hour and includes all delays.

OVERALL TIME - The time of travel, including stops and delays except those off the traveled way.

P

PARALLEL PARKING - Parking where the longitudinal axis of vehicles are parallel to alignment of the roadway so that the vehicles are facing in the same direction as the movement of adjacent vehicular traffic.

PARKING DURATION - Length of time a vehicle is parked.

PASSENGER VEHICLE - A free-wheeled, self-propelled vehicle designed for the transportation of persons but limited in seating capacity to not more than seven passengers, not including the driver. It includes taxicabs, limousines, and station wagons, but does not include motorcycles. (In capacity studies, also includes light reconnaissance vehicles, and pickup trucks.)

PASSENGER (TRANSIT) VOLUME - The total number of public transit occupants being transported in a period of time.

PEAK PERIOD - That portion of the day in which maximum traffic volumes are experienced.

PEDESTRIAN - Any person afoot. For purpose of accident classification, this will be interpreted to include any person riding in or upon a device moved or designed for movement by human power or the force of gravity, except bicycles, including stilts, skates, skis, sleds, toy wagons, and scooters.

PERCENT OF GRADE - The slope in the longitudinal direction of the pavement expressed in percent which is the number of units of change in elevation per 100 units of horizontal distance.

PERCENT OF GREEN TIME - The percentage of green time allotted to the direction of travel being studies.

PROPERTY DAMAGE - Damage to property as a result of a motor vehicle accident that may be a basis of a claim for compensation. Does not include compensation for loss of life or for personal injuries.

PUBLIC HIGHWAYS- The entire width between property lines, or boundary lines, of every way or place of which any part is open to use of the public for purposes of vehicular traffic as a matter of right or custom.

PUBLIC TRANSIT - The public passenger carryi ng service afforded by vehicles following regular routes and making specified stops.

R

REFLECTORIZE - The application of some material to traffic control devices or hazards which will return to the eyes of the road user some portion of the light from his vehicle headlights, thereby producing a brightness which attracts attention.

REGULATORY DEVICE - A device used to indicate the required method of traffic movement or use of the public traffic way.

REGULATORY SIGN - A sign used to indicate the required method of traffic movement or use of the traffic way.

RIGHT TURN LANE - A lane within the normal surfaced width reserved for right turning vehicles.

ROADWAY - That portion of a traffic way including shoulders, improved, designed, or ordinarily used for vehicle traffic.

S

SEPARATE TURNING LANE - Added traffic lane which is separated from the intersection area by an island or unpaved area. It may be wide enough for one or two line operation

SHOULDER - The portion of the roadway contiguous with the traveled way for accommodation of stopped vehicles, for emergency use, and for lateral support of base and surface courses.

SIGHT DISTANCES - The length of roadway visible to the driver of a passenger vehicle at any given point on the roadway when the view is unobstructed by traffic.

SIGNAL CYCLE - The total time required for one complete sequence of the intervals of a traffic signal.

SIGNAL CONTROLLER - A complete electrical mechanism for controlling the operation of traffic control signals, including the timer and all necessary auxiliary apparatus mounted in a cabinet.

SIGNAL FACE - That part of a signal head provided for controlling traffic from a single direction.

SIGNAL HEAD - An assembly containing one or more signal faces that may be designated accordingly as one-way, two-way, multi-way.

SIGNAL PHASE - A part of the total time cycle allocated to movements receiving the right-of-way or to any combination ments receiving the right-of-way simultaneously during one

SIMPLE INTERSECTION - An intersection of two traffic ways, approaches.

SPEED - The rate of movement of a vehicle, generally expressed in miles per hour.

STOPPING SIGHT DISTANCE –The distance required by a drive of a vehicle, given speed, to bring vehicle to a stop after and object becomes visible.

STREET WIDTH - The width of the paved or traveled portion of the roadway.

T

THROUGH MOVEMENT - (See THROUGH TRAFFIC)

THROUGH STREET - A street on which traffic is given the right-of-way so that vehicles entering or crossing the street must yield the right-of-way.

THROUGH TRAFFIC - Traffic proceeding through a military installation or portion not originating in or destined to that military installation or portion thereof.

TIME CYCLE - (See SIGNAL CYCLE)

TRAFFIC - Pedestrians, ridden or herded animals, vehicles, street cars, and other conveyances, either singly or together, while using any street for purposes of travel.

TRAFFIC ACCIDENT - Any accident involving a motor vehicle in motion that results in death, injury, or property damage.

TRAFFIC ACTUATED CONTROLLER- An automatic controller for supervising the operation of traffic control signals in accordance with the immediate and varying demands of traffic as registered with the-controller by means of detectors.

TRAFFIC CONTROL - All measures except those of a structural kind that serve to control and guide traffic and to promote road safety.

TRAFFIC CONTROL DEVICE - A Traffic control device is any sign, signal, marking, or device placed or erected for the purpose of regulating, warning, or guiding traffic.

TRAFFIC DEMAND - The volume of traffic desiring to use a particular route or facility.

TRAFFIC ENGINEERING - That phase of engineering that deals with the planning and geometric design of streets, highways, and abutting lands, and with traffic operations thereon, as their use is related to the safe, convenient, and economic transportation of persons and goods.

TRAFFIC FLOW - The movement of vehicles on a roadway.

TRAFFIC FLOW PATTERN - The distribution of traffic volumes on a street or highway network~

TRAFFIC GENERATOR - A traffic producing area such as a post exchange, parking lot, or administrative center.

TRAFFIC SIGNAL INTERVAL - Anyone of the several divisions of the total time cycle during which signal indications do not change.

TRAFFICWAY - The entire width between property lines (or other boundary lines) of every way or place of which any part is open to use of public for purposes of vehicular traffic as a matter of right or custom.

TRANSIT VEHICLE - A passenger carrying vehicle, such as a bus or streetcar which follows regular routes and makes specific stops.

TRAVEL TIME- The total elapsed time from the origin to destination of a trip.

TURNING MOVEMENT - The traffic making a designated turn at an intersection.

TWO-WAY STREETS - A street on which traffic may move in opposite directions simultaneously. It may be either divided or undivided.

TYPE OF ACCIDENT - The kind of motor vehicle accident, such as head-on, right-angle, etc.

TYPE OF SURFACE - The class of surface such as concrete, asphalt, gravel, etc.

U

UNINTERRRUPTED FLOW - The flow of-vehicles under ideal conditions resulting in unrestricted movement.

V

VEHICLE - Every device in, upon, or by which any person or property is or may be transported or drawn upon a highway, except those devices moved by human power or used exclusively upon stationary rails or tracks.

VEHICULE OCCUPANCY - The average number of occupants per automobile, including the driver.

VOLUME - The number of vehicles passing a given point during a specified period of time.

W

WARNING SIGN - A sign used to indicate conditions that are actually or potentially hazardous to highway users.

WARRANT - Formally stated conditions that have been accepted as minimum requirements for justifying installation of a traffic control device or regulation.

Z

ZONE (ORIGIN-DESTINATION STUDIES) -- A division of an area established for the purpose of analyzing origin-destination studies. It may be bounded by physical barriers such as rivers and highways, or may be the location of individual work organizations that have duty stations in relatively close proximity.

DEFINITIONS OF UNIFORM TRAFFIC CONTROL TERMS

TABLE OF CONTENTS

	Page
SECTION 1 – Definition of Words and Phrases	1
2 – General Definitions	1
3 – Definitions Relating to Signs	3
4 – Definitions Relating to Markings	3
5 – Definitions Relating to Signals	4
6 – Definitions Relating to Islands	5
7 – Definitions Relating to Construction and Maintenance Traffic Controls	5

DEFINITIONS OF UNIFORM TRAFFIC CONTROL TERMS

1. Definition of Words and Phrases

    The words and phrases defined in the following sections shall, for the purpose of the section, have the meanings respectively ascribed to them in this part except when the context otherwise requires.

2. General Definitions

    1. Authorized Emergency Vehicle—Such fire department vehicles, police vehicles and ambulances as are publicly owned, and such other publicly or privately owned vehicles as designated by the public body or official having jurisdiction.
    2. Crosswalk
    (a) That part of a roadway at an intersection included within the connections of the lateral lines of the sidewalks on opposite sides of the highway measured from the curbs or in the absence of curbs, from the edges of the traversable roadway;
    (b) Any portion of a roadway at an intersection or elsewhere distinctly indicated for pedestrian crossing by lines or other markings on the surface.
    3. Curb—A vertical or sloping member generally along and defining the edge of a roadway.
    4. Curb line—The boundary between a roadway and a sidewalk, usually marked by a curb.
    5. District, Business—The territory contiguous to and including a highway, when within any 600 feet along such highway there are buildings in use for business or industrial purposes, including but not limited to hotels, banks, or office buildings, railroad stations, and public buildings which occupy at least 300 feet of frontage on one side or 300 feet collectively on both sides of the highway.
    6. District, Residence—The territory contiguous to and including a highway not comprising a business district when the property on such highway for a distance of 300 feet or more is in the main improved with residences or residences and buildings in use for business.
    7. District, Rural—Any territory not included in a business or residence district as defined herein, whether or not within the boundaries of a municipality.
    8. District, Urban—The territory contiguous to and including any street which is built up with structures devoted to business, industry or dwelling houses situated at intervals of less than 100 feet for a distance of a quarter of a mile or more.
    9. Expressway—A divided arterial highway for through traffic with partial control of access and generally with grade separations at major intersections.
    10. Freeway—An expressway with full control of access.
    11. Gore—The area immediately beyond the bifurcation of two roadways, bounded by the edges of those roadways.
    12. Highway (or Street)—The entire width between the boundary lines of every way, publicly maintained, when any part thereof is open to the use of the public for purposes of vehicular travel.
    13. Highway, Arterial—Any U.S. or State numbered route, controlled access highway, or other major radial or circumferential street or highway designated by local authorities within their respective jurisdictions as part of a major arterial system of streets or highways.

14. Highway, Controlled-Access—Every highway, street, or roadway in respect to which owners or occupants of abutting lands and other persons have no legal right of access to or from the same except at such points only and in such manner as may be determined by the public authority having jurisdiction over such highway, street, or roadway.
15. Highway, Divided—A highway with separate roadways for traffic in opposite directions.
16. Highway, Major—The roadway approach or approaches at an intersection normally carrying the major volume of vehicular traffic.
17. Highway, Minor—The roadway approach or approaches at an intersection normally carrying the minor volume of vehicular traffic.
18. Highway, Through—A highway or portion thereof on which vehicular traffic is given preferential right-of-way, and at the entrances to which vehicular traffic from intersecting highways is required by law to yield the right-of-way to vehicles on such through highway in obedience to a stop sign, yield sign, or other official traffic control device, when such signs or devices are erected as provided by law.
19. Intersection—

    (a) The area embraced within the prolongation or connection of the lateral curb lines, or, if none, then the lateral boundary lines of the roadways of two highways which join one another at, or approximately at, right angles, or the area within which vehicles traveling upon different highways joining at any other angle may come in conflict.

    (b) Where a highway includes two roadways (30) feet or more apart, then every crossing of each roadway of such divided highway by an intersecting highway shall be regarded as a separate intersection. In the event such intersecting highway also includes two roadways (30) feet or more apart, then every crossing of two roadways of such highways shall be regarded as a separate intersection.

    (c) The junction of an alley with a street or highway shall not constitute an intersection.
20. Median—The portion of a divided highway separating the traveled ways for traffic in opposite direction.
21. No Passing Zone—A section of highway designated by the public body or official having jurisdiction as one where overtaking and passing or driving to the left of the roadway would be especially hazardous.
22. Official Traffic Control Devices (or Traffic Control Devices)— All traffic signs, highway traffic signals, traffic markings, and other devices erected or placed on or adjacent to a highway or street by authority of the public body or official having jurisdiction, for the purpose of regulating, warning, or guiding traffic.
23. Pavement—That part of a roadway having a constructed surface for the facilitation of vehicular traffic.
24. Pedestrian—Any person afoot.
25. Ramp—An inclined section of way over which traffic passes for the primary purpose of ascending or descending so as to make connections with other ways. Also, an interconnecting roadway of a traffic interchange, or any connection between highway facilities of different levels, on which vehicles may enter or leave a designated highway.
26. Right-of-Way—The right of one vehicle or pedestrian to proceed in a lawful manner in preference to another vehicle or pedestrian approaching under such circumstances of direction, speed and proximity as to give rise to danger of collision unless one grants precedence to the other.

27. Roadway—That portion of a highway improved, designed, or ordinarily used for vehicular travel, exclusive of the berm or shoulder. In the event a highway includes two or more separate roadways, the term "roadway," as used herein, refers to any such roadway separately but not to all such roadways collectively.
28. Shoulder—The portion of the roadway contiguous with the traveled way for accommodations of stopped vehicles, for emergency use, and for lateral support of base and surface courses.
29. Sidewalk—That portion of a street between the curb lines, or the lateral line of a roadway, and the adjacent property lines, intended for the use of pedestrians.
30. Street—(See highway).
31. Traffic—Pedestrians, ridden or herded animals, vehicles, streetcars, and other conveyances either singly or together while using any highway for purposes of travel.
32. Traffic Lane—A strip of roadway intended to accommodate the forward movement of a single line of vehicles.
33. Vehicle—Every device in, upon, or by which any person or property is or may be transported or drawn upon a highway, except devices moved by human power or used exclusively upon stationary rails or tracks.

3. Definitions Relating to Signs

   1. Guide Sign—A sign used to show route designations, destinations, directions, distances, services, points of interest, and other geographical or cultural information.
   2. Lane-Use Sign—A sign indicating regulations governing use of specific lanes.
   3. Legend—Word messages or symbols used on signs to cover specific meanings.
   4. Public Parking Area (or Facility)—A parking facility available for use by the general public, with or without payment of a fee.
   5. Regulatory Sign—A sign used to give notice of traffic laws or regulations.
   6. Traffic Sign (or Sign)—A device mounted on a fixed or portable support whereby a specific message is conveyed by means of words or symbols placed or erected for the purpose of regulating, warning, or guiding traffic.
   7. Warning Sign—A sign used to give notice of conditions on, or adjacent to, a highway or street that are potentially hazardous to traffic operations.

4. Definitions Relating to Markings

   1. Barrier Line—A line which, when placed parallel to a center or lane line, or to another barrier line, indicates that all traffic must not cross the line for purposes of overtaking and passing.
   2. Center Line—A line indicating the division of the roadway between traffic traveling in opposite directions.
   3. Channelizing Line—A line which directs traffic and indicates that traffic should not cross but may proceed on either side.
   4. Delineator—A light-reflecting device mounted at the side of the roadway, in series with others, to indicate the alignment of the roadway.
   5. Edge Line—A line which indicates the edge of the roadway.
   6. Lane Line—A line separating two lanes of traffic traveling in the same direction.
   7. Object Markings—Markings intended for use on obstructions within or adjacent to the roadway.
   8. Pavement Markings—Markings set into the surface of, applied upon, or attached to the pavement.

9. Stop Line (or Limit Line)—A line which indicates where vehicles should stop when directed by a traffic officer or traffic control device.
10. Traffic Markings (or Markings)—All lines, patterns, words, colors, or other devices, except signs and power-operated traffic control devices, set into the surface of, applied upon, or attached to the pavement or curbing or to objects within or adjacent to the roadway, placed for the purpose of regulating, warning, or guiding traffic.

5. Definitions Relating to Signals

   1. Back-Plates—A strip of thin material extending outward parallel to the signal face on all sides of a signal housing to provide suitable background for the signal indications.
   2. Controller—A complete electrical mechanism mounted in a cabinet for controlling the operation of a traffic control signal.
   3. Detector—A device by which vehicles, streetcars, trolley buses, or pedestrians are enabled to register their presence with a traffic-actuated controller.
   4. Highway Traffic Signal—Any power-operated traffic-control device, except a sign or a barricade warning light, or steady burning electric lamps, by which traffic is warned or is directed to take some specific action.
   5. Interval—Any one of the several divisions of the time cycle during which signal indications do not change.
   6. Lane—Use Control SignalA highway traffic signal which is erected to control the direction of vehicular traffic movement in an individual lane.
   7. Major Street—The roadway approach or approaches at an intersection normally carrying the major volume of vehicular traffic.
   8. Minor Street—The roadway approach or approaches at an intersection normally carrying the minor volume of vehicular traffic.
   9. Optical Unit—An assembly of a lens, reflector, light source, and other components if required, with the necessary supporting parts to be used for providing a signal indication.
   10. Pedestrian Detector—A detector, usually of the push-button type, installed near the roadway capable of being operated by hand.
   11. Pedestrian Signal—A traffic control signal which is erected for the exclusive purpose of directing pedestrian traffic at signalized locations.
   12. Pedestrian Signal Indication—The illumination of a pedestrian signal lens or equivalent device.
   13. Pretimed Signal—A type of traffic control signal which operates on predetermined scheduled time cycles and intervals.
   14. Signal Face—That part of a traffic control signal provided for controlling one or more traffic movements in a single direction. Turning indications may be included in a signal face.
   15. Signal Head—An assembly containing one or more signal faces.
   16. Signal Indication—The illumination of a traffic control signal lens or equivalent device.
   17. Signal Installation—All of the equipment and material involved in the control of traffic at one intersection by a traffic control signal.
   18. Signal Lens—That part of the optical unit which redirects the light coming directly from the light source and its reflector, if any.
   19. Signal Support—The physical means whereby a signal head is supported in a particular location.

20. Signal System—Two or more signal installations operating in coordination.
21. Time Cycle—The time period required for one complete sequence of signal indications.
22. Traffic-Actuated Signal—A type of traffic control signal in which the intervals are varied in accordance with the demands of traffic as registered by the actuation of detectors.
23. Traffic Control Signal (Traffic Signal)—A type of highway traffic signal, manually, electrically, or mechanically operated by which traffic is alternately directed to stop and permitted to proceed.
24. Traffic Phase—A part of the time cycle allocated to any traffic movement receiving the right-of-way or to any combination of traffic movements receiving the right-of-way simultaneously during one or more intervals.
25. Train-Approach Signal—A highway traffic signal which indicates to highway traffic, the approach and passage of railroad trains at a railroad-highway grade crossing.
26. Vehicular Phase—A traffic phase allocated to all traffic except pedestrians.

6. Definitions Relating to Islands

   1. Approach End—An end of an island or area between roadways which faces approaching traffic passing to one or both sides.
   2. Buffer—A structure at the approach end of a safety zone designed to deflect or stop any vehicle which collides with it.
   3. Island—(Traffic Island)—An area within a roadway from which vehicular traffic is intended to be excluded, together with any area at the approach thereto occupied by warning devices.
   4. Island, Channelizing—A traffic island located in a roadway area to control and direct specific movements of traffic to definite channels.
   5. Island, Divisional—A traffic island used to separate traffic moving in the same or opposite directions.
   6. Island, Pedestrian Refuge—An island designed for the use and protection of pedestrians.
   7. Raised Bars—A series of bars extending above the normal pavement surface to make any wheel encroachment obvious to a vehicle operator without loss of control of the vehicle.
   8. Button—A rounded object extending above the normal pavement surface for the purpose of channelizing traffic movement.

7. Definitions Relating to Construction and Maintenance Traffic Controls

   1. Barricade—A portable or fixed barrier having object markings, used to close all or a portion of the right-of-way to vehicular traffic.
   2. Barricade Warning Light—A portable, power-operated, lens directed, enclosed light used in either the steady burn or flashing mode to mark obstructions or hazards in construction and maintenance work areas.
   3. Steady Burning Electric Lamps—A series of low wattage, yellow electric lamps used to mark obstructions or hazards in construction and maintenance work areas.